To Judith,
May your journey be filled
with wisdom, love and joy!
Blessings, Nancy Heha & Jane Treat

"Absolutely beautiful! I laughed. I cried and I nodded my head saying, 'Oh, yes!"

~ Polly Treat

"It is a beautiful book! You have done a great job of making this a true journey of learning ... I am enthralled... Awesome!"

~ Renee Fajardo, JD

"What an inspiring book! I felt like I was right there with each person telling their story ... climbing their mountains. This book touched my soul!"

~ Anne Childs

"This book is beautifully written and shows a deep understanding of what Middlehood women need and want to hear."

~ Sally Douglas

WOMEN
&
MIDDLEHOOD

Halfway Up the Mountain

Jane Treat
&
Nancy Geha, Ed.D.

BALBOA
PRESS
A DIVISION OF HAY HOUSE

Balboa Press books may be ordered through booksellers or by contacting:

Balboa Press
A Division of Hay House
1663 Liberty Drive
Bloomington, IN 47403
www.balboapress.com
1-(877) 407-4847

Printed in the United States of America.

Library of Congress Control Number: 2013911704

ISBN: 978-1-4525-7713-5 (sc)
ISBN: 978-1-4525-7715-9 (hc)
ISBN: 978-1-4525-7714-2 (e)

Balboa Press rev. date: 07/11/2013

DEDICATIONS

From Nancy

To my Momma, Allene Marie Deel Geha, an angel on earth and now in heaven. Her example of how to live life to the fullest with love, patience, kindness, and humor will stay in my heart forever. I love you "millions and billions and trillions, one hundred million times over."

To my sister, Linda Sue, who lived more in her twenty-one years than most people live in a lifetime. Her sweetness, love, and kindness will always live in my heart. I love you, sweet Linda.

To my aunt Dee Paulich, whose love of family and zest for life are a wonder and a miracle. I love you with all my heart.

To my aunt Nay Kanascky, who has always been there for me and whose love of family is truly a blessing. I love you with all my heart.

From Jane

For my mother, Mary Ellen Shannon Treat;
my grandmothers, Catharine Emery Shannon
and Madeleine Moore Treat;
and all of my other ancestors who I follow up the mountain trail.
Thank you for showing me the way.

TABLE OF CONTENTS

PREFACE

WE STARTED THINKING ABOUT THIS BOOK when we were both in our early fifties. At that time, our lives were filled with terrific friends, good relationships, wonderful creative work, and lots of adventures. In addition, we also had demanding jobs, elderly and ailing parents, dying friends, changing family relationships, and a variety of perimenopause/menopause issues. Like many women our age, we felt strong and good in some areas, and confused and overwhelmed in others.

We got a copy of Dr. Christiane Northrup's book, *The Wisdom of Menopause*, and started reading the chapters about our specific perimenopause/menopause challenges. We felt encouraged and comforted to find out that there was nothing "wrong" with us, and that there were many things we could do to help our bodies and emotions through this time. As we talked to our sisters and friends, we heard the same sorts of worries and questions from them, and realized that all of us could use some encouragement. So the idea for the book was born.

Both of us had worked for many years in our respective careers: Nancy as a motivational speaker, workshop leader, teacher, public health professional, and nurse; and Jane as a storyteller, rites-of-passage guide, writer, public school media coordinator and community organizer. Much of what we had taught others through our work suddenly seemed applicable to women at this time of life. We brought the best of what we had learned from our teachers and mentors, and then searched back through our own work to add the best of that material into the mix.

As we thought about topics for the book, we decided not to read other books on women and menopause, women and aging, or women in middle age. Instead, we kept asking our sisters and women friends how they felt and what helped them as they lived through all their life changes. Ultimately, we created a questionnaire and sent it to many Middlehood women we knew. They answered it and then passed it on, and we began to hear back from women who lived all over the United States and several other countries. They were from diverse backgrounds and cultures, as well as from many religious/spiritual paths or no spiritual path at all. While we collected other women's experiences and thoughts, we also began to explore our own stories. We were astonished at how many experiences we all shared, despite the differences in the details of our lives.

The heart of the book began to emerge. We quickly understood what it was *not* going to be. It was not going to be a book on middle-age beauty and health. It was also not going to be a handbook with step-by-step procedures for surviving our middle years. We are committed to social justice and wanted women to be active with their concerns and communities, but it was not going to be a guide to making political change. Rather, we wanted to gather wisdom from real women that could offer encouragement to fully explore our Middlehood and its possibilities. We did not ignore the real difficulties and painful situations that many of us face, but we chose to focus on growing the positive aspects of this time of our lives. Finally, we chose to write the book from the point of view of "we" as a way of acknowledging the power of our shared experiences.

Now approaching sixty, we reflect on the last almost twenty years and realize what a transformative time it has been. We personally lived every chapter of the book before or while we were writing it! We are grateful for all of the women who told their stories—some, our dearest family and friends, and others, women we have never met but know, by our shared stories, have walked a similar road.

We are all authorities on our own lives, and from that place, we know there is no one way or one answer for all of us. We also know that Middlehood women, rich with creative ideas and insights from our life experiences, offer so much that could be helpful to others. To paraphrase the old expression, we have to do the work ourselves, but we do not have to do it alone.

Here in Middlehood is an opportunity to dig deep into our lives and sort out our pasts while we prepare for our futures. We hope that this book will be a helpful tool as you assess, experiment, self-reflect, and take action. Perhaps it will spark conversations or inspire new ideas and questions as you navigate through the challenging and joyous time of Middlehood.

Blessings,
Nancy and Jane

ACKNOWLEDGMENTS AND PERMISSIONS

From Jane

As I write this, I'm listening to the birds, watching the sky, and hoping for rain. I feel the power of the Spirit and I know I am blessed.

How can I thank Nancy Geha, my coauthor and partner? You are one of the true motivating forces in my universe, providing love, support, creative ideas, and dynamic energy. You keep me moving when I stall, prop me up when I fall down, and feed my sometimes wavering belief that what we do matters! You are a precious gift.

Thank you to my parents, Mary Ellen and Paul Treat, for the great gifts of life, love, and the willingness to go on the adventure, every time. And to my sisters, Polly and Paige Treat, thank you for the past and the present, and for the realization that I only love you more the older we get! To all the rest of my extended family, I love you all.

My profound love and appreciation to Ann and Dick Rundall, who have opened doors and offered generosity, encouragement, and love for more than forty years.

A lifetime of thanks to Meredith Little and Steven Foster, who saw me and believed in me back when I was looking for the trail, and who gave me some of the most important tools of my life.

My deep gratitude to Reneé O'Connor, Sandra Wilson, Cindy Lollar, and Susan McCarn Gambill for your stories. It would take days to explain what they have meant to me over the years, but they have made all the difference in my life. Your willingness to share your struggles, fears, and strength gives us courage and clarity in our own mountain journeys.

Hugs and thanks to Renee Fajardo for supporting us and this book, years before it was even finished.

More hugs and thanks to Pam Faro and Susan Kaplan, who read, commented, and shared stories. You always give me new eyes to see what is deep, rich, and full of love, just as you are.

To Pat Robinson, friend and sometime traveling companion in every way, thank you for your incredible call to excellence, and the willingness to read and share your thoughts.

To Lucille Kinlein, my "wise woman," who knew there was a book in me before I knew it. Thank you for teaching me to keep my eye on what is alive and moving.

From Nancy

First and foremost, I am grateful to God for giving us the strength, patience, wisdom, and love to write this book. His divine love was with us every step of the way.

Love, thanks, and hugs to my coauthor and partner, Jane Treat, without whom this book would not have been possible. Your love, support, and incredible patience with me over the years have been a gift from God. You are my rock and touchstone in life.

To my beloved parents, William (Bill) and Allene Geha, whose unconditional love, support, and encouragement throughout my life have been an extraordinary blessing. Although you are no longer here on this earth, you are my angels in heaven.

A huge thank you, love and hugs to my sweet sister, Sally Douglas, who has been a great gift to me, and whose love, humor, and support have gotten me through many difficult times. You are my angel and the source of strength that God has given me every day of my life.

Thank you to my brothers and sisters who have loved and supported me over the years. You are so important and special to me and I love you with all my heart. Thank you and love to my nieces, nephews, and great-nieces for your love and kindness.

Thank you to Anne Childs, not only a dear friend but an incredible editor and reader. I am grateful for your support and encouragement, and for taking the time to provide feedback and share your funny stories. I so appreciate you.

Thank you to Sharon Tracey, my dear friend, who offered such incredible perspectives about the diversity of Middlehood women. You are amazing.

From Both of Us

Thank you to Teresa Sprecher, our longtime friend, webmaster, graphic designer, sounding board, and confidante before, during, and forever after this process. You are amazing and loved.

We are so grateful to Meredith Little and Steven Foster for the use of your simple but powerful tool, the Equation for Transformation. We hope that others will find it as helpful as we have.

A huge thank you to all of you who shared your wonderful stories and quotes, and gave us a small piece of yourself to love and cherish. We will always treasure your words of wisdom.

At every milestone in life and at the conclusion of every creative work, we are overwhelmed with gratitude for all of the family and friends who have been part of our lives. We find it incredibly difficult to limit our appreciation and acknowledgments because we know the roots of relationships go very deep, and there is no untangling how woven together we all are. In an effort to keep this section from running into hundreds of pages, let us say this: if we have known you and loved you, then you are in our hearts, and we are grateful.

Permissions

We are grateful to all the following individuals/authors for sharing their work and the use of their quotations, which inspire and motivate others to live life with meaning and purpose.

Ana Nogales, Ph.D., with permission, interview with Ana Nogales as published in *Para Todos,* www.ananogales.com, www.casadelafamilia.org.

Anna Quindlen, © 2005 Quotation taken from *Being Perfect.*

Anne Lamott, with permission by author, *Bird by Bird, Operating Instructions, and Traveling Mercies.*

Audre Lorde, *The Cancer Journals*, copyright, 1980. By permission of Aunt Lute Books, www.auntlute.com.

Barbara De Angelis, Ph.D., with permission, *Chicken Soup for the Couple's Soul: Inspirational Stories about Love and Relationship*, www.barbaradeangelis.com.

Brené Brown, Ph.D., LMSW, with permission, author of *Daring Greatly*, www.brenebrown.com.

Caroline Myss, Ph.D., with permission, www.myss.com.

Christiane Northrup, MD, Reprinted with permission from *The Wisdom of Menopause: Creating Physical and Emotional Health and Healing During the Change*, copyright 2012, by Christiane Northrup, MD.

Cindy Lollar, with permission.

Ellen DeGeneres, www.ellentv.com.

Georgia O'Keeffe, with permission from the Georgia O'Keeffe Museum, www.okeeffemuseum.org.

Iyanla Vanzant, with permission, *Iyanla: Fix My Life* on OWN: Oprah Winfrey Network, www.iyanlavanzant.com.

Jean Shinoda Bolen, M.D., with permission by author, *Crones Don't Whine: Concentrated Wisdom for Juicy Women* (Boston: Conari Press, 2003), www.jeanbolen.com.

Judy Baca, with permission, UCLA Commencement Address 2012 School Of Art and Architecture, www.judybaca.com, sparcmurals.org.

June Jordan, "Poem About South African Women" by June Jordan from *Directed by Desire: The Collected Poems of June Jordan*. Reprinted with the permission of the June M. Jordan Literary Estate Trust, and Copper Canyon Press, www.junejordan.com.

Linda Hogan, with permission by author and W.W. Norton and Company, *Woman Who Watches Over the World: A Native Memoir*, (New York: W.W. Norton and Company, 2002).

M. Lucille Kinlein, with permission, Founder of the Profession and Practice of Kinlein, www.kinlein.org.

Mae C. Jemison, MD, with permission, Dorothy Jemison Foundation for Excellence, www.jemisonfoundation.org.

Martha Lanier, with permission by author, *Pink Lemonade: Mastectomy Tips and Insights from a Breast Cancer Survivor*, (2009), www.marthalanier.com.

Mary Anne Radmacher, with permission by author and Conari Press, *Courage Doesn't Always Roar*, (San Francisco, Conari Press, 2009), www.maryanneradmacher.com.

Meredith Little, with permission, for the use of the *Equation For Transformation*, School of Lost Borders, www.schooloflostborders.org.

Mohja Kahf, Ph.D., by permission of the author. From the poem, 'The Woman Dear to Herself" in *E-mails from Scheherazad*, a poetry book from University Press of Florida, Contemporary Poetry Series, 2003.

Naomi Shihab Nye, by permission of the author, 2013. From "Kindness" in *Words Under the Words*, (Oregon: Far Corner Books, 1995).

Patty Montgomery, with permission by author, *Mythmaking: Heal Your Past, Claim Your Future*, Sibyl Publications, copyright 1994, for Cynthia Henry, author of the *The Lost Purr*.

Pema Chödrön, with permission, Pema Chödrön Foundation, www.pemachodronfoundation.org.

Rachel Naomi Remen, M.D., quoted from *My Grandfather's Blessings: Stories of Strength, Refuge and Belonging* by Rachel Naomi Remen MD, with permission by author, www.rachelremen.com.

Reneé O'Connor, with permission, www.rocpictures.com, www.reneeoconnor.net.

Rita Rudner, with permission, www.ritafunny.com.

Sandra Wilson, by permission.

Thanks to Sarah Ban Breathnach, author of *Simple Abundance: A Daybook of Comfort and Joy*, (New York: Grand Central Publishing, 1995).

Susan McCarn Gambill, with permission.

Suzan-Lori Parks, with permission, Commencement Address, Mount Holyoke, 2001.

Suzanne Willis Zoglio, with permission by author, *Create a Life That Tickles Your Soul*, www.tickleyoursoul.com.

Violet Trefusis's Letters to Vita Sackville-West ©Copyright by Tiziana Masucci. We wish to thank Tiziana Masucci for permission to quote from the letter of Violet Trefusis. For information on Violet Trefusis and new editions of her books, visit: www.violettrefusis.com.

Wilma Mankiller, Northeastern State University, Tahlequah OK, Spring 2009 Commencement Speech, with permission by Fulcrum Publishing.

INTRODUCTION

When I dare to be powerful, to use my strength in the service of my vision, then it becomes less and less important whether I am afraid.

~ Audre Lorde, *The Cancer Journals*

IS AGE REALLY JUST A STATE of mind? Is forty actually the new thirty? Does life honestly begin at forty? Is it true that we are only as young as we feel? Whether we love or hate those expressions, they say a lot about our individual and collective need to find some peace with getting older, and forty is a significant milestone in that process.

Whether we are happy and healthy at forty or depressed by even the idea of it, there is something about hitting the big 4-0 that prompts most of us to reflect a bit on our first four decades. Some of us may be quite pleased with what we find, while others may be frustrated that we seem to be nowhere and have wasted so much time. Either way, the average life expectancy for a woman in the early twenty-first century is eighty; that makes forty the midpoint.

From now on, the number of years behind us grows larger, and the number in front of us, smaller. Whether or not we are content with our lives, this fact creates subtle changes that grow more pronounced every year as we pass into our fifties and sixties, heading for the enormous milestone of sixty-five.

The years between forty and sixty-five are a generation of change. At forty, most of us probably look good, feel strong and healthy, and are likely in the midst of major family and work activities. In our fifties, most of our children are grown or nearly so, menopause is looming, and we may be taking care of elderly parents while still working full-time. By the time we reach sixty-five, our lives, concerns, and expectations have changed significantly. Now many of us are beginning retirement and enjoying grandchildren, and nearly all of us are saying good-bye to loved ones as they pass away. It is a long way from forty to sixty-five, but society tells us that forty is where the middle years begin, and sixty-five is where they end.

This book is an exploration and celebration of how women journey through these middle years. It draws upon one of the most powerful methods that many of us use to negotiate the chapters and challenges in our lives: we share our stories and experiences with other women. Whether over a cup of coffee with a sister or a glass of wine with a coworker, over a table full of dirty dishes with an old friend or on a Tuesday night phone call with our moms, we can talk to each other about nearly anything! This is where we cried through the story of a broken heart or laughed hysterically through the tale of a childhood adventure. We probably consulted our moms about how to get a new baby to sleep through the night, and these days, a friend may have a remedy for hot flashes. A lifetime of women have listened and offered wisdom, laughter, and love. We may look back through the years to find that some of the most inspiring and therapeutic conversations we have ever had were these informal heart-to-hearts with women we love.

Many women contributed to this book with their stories, experiences, and insights on topics that are relevant to Middlehood women: our changing bodies and relationships; the loss of loved ones; the spectrum of work issues; redefining our sense of beauty and attractiveness; how to deepen our sense of authenticity; the power of our accumulated wisdom; and tools for letting go of old patterns and ways of thinking. Telling our own stories has always given us new understandings, but our stories can also enrich someone else's life by offering inspiration, guidance, and a different perspective. Think of the wealth of experience each of us has to offer, and then think of the well of wisdom we draw from when we combine the insights from many women and their stories.

Every single one of us has tried and failed or tried and succeeded at something important to us. We have successfully faced fears, obstacles, addictions, or disabling circumstances. We have survived cancer, given birth, or held the hand of a precious person as they passed out of this world. And we have worked—oh, how we have worked—at everything from raising children and growing food to creating beauty, teaching people to read, and fighting for justice and equality. All our lives contain the same themes—birth, death, love, loss, challenge, victory, sacrifice, and unexpected gifts—that are included in every great story ever told. In telling these stories, we give meaning to the experiences of our past, shape the course of our future, and encourage someone else to walk their path with strength and courage.

Three themes of inner work emerge through the tools and stories in this book, and each offers opportunities to grow in ways that enhance and deepen our lives and experiences. First, we can commit to being authentic and living the truth of who we are to the best of our ability. Second, we can reach deep and find the courage to walk our true path and to face the challenges that appear. Third, we can make peace, or at least allow a peaceful coexistence, with our inner conflicts. We have already spent more than half our lives learning these lessons, and they are not easy. But these life lessons are important and reflect our accumulating wisdom.

So how will we proceed through the coming years? Will we be depressed by the challenges and changes of this time, or will we celebrate the amazing new accomplishments and skills we gain? We hope that this book will encourage all of us to explore our lives and help us journey up our mountains with courage, strength, and humor.

CHAPTER 1

Middlehood

We begin to find and become ourselves when we notice how we are already found, already truly, entirely, wildly, messily, marvelously who we were born to be.

~ Anne Lamott

Don't let anyone rob you of your imagination, your creativity, or your curiosity. It's your place in the world; it's your life. Go on and do all you can with it, and make it the life you want to live.

~ Mae C. Jemison

Who Are We?

WOMEN BETWEEN THE AGES OF FORTY and sixty-five are a force to be reckoned with! We are many; we are powerful; and we do not fit in any box. We come from such diverse backgrounds, experiences, and expectations that we could never identify them all. The words we choose to describe this time are vivid and strong, and as varied as we are. We use verbs like endure, juggle, create, achieve, survive, energize, struggle, and persevere; and adjectives like courageous, overwhelmed, thrilled, intense, exhausted, vigorous, and triumphant. What we share is the power and the challenge of this phase of life.

In many cultures, this period of time is a prelude to the attaining of wisdom and respect that comes in elderhood. But for those of us who do not live in such cultures, confusion reigns. One moment, we may feel healthier and happier than we have ever been, more fulfilled and truly ourselves; thirty minutes later, on our third trip up the stairs for something we forgot, we have no idea where we are in our life and have completely lost our sense of balance. Most of us probably manage to combine this clarity and disorientation as we actively struggle with the push and pull of this time in our lives.

How did we get to this time of contradictions? It may seem that just last week, we were young, with our whole life ahead of us. Then we woke up one morning to find that everything had changed. It could have started with such simple things as a young adult calling us "ma'am" or a small child referring to us as "that old lady." Maybe it was the day we patiently waited and waited at a counter while a young clerk was busy with everyone else, and started to wonder when we had become invisible. Or most of us, if pressed, would confess to a day when we started to pull out our gray hairs in an attempt to postpone the inevitable. These startling moments are often the precursors to a time of profound change that is coming whether we like it or not. Our middle years are upon us!

What Is It?

Middlehood. It's not found in the dictionary, so why did we coin it to describe the middle years of our lives? What is wrong with the word *middle-aged*? The simple answer is that, when we look at how language reflects culture and values, we see that *middle-aged* is too small, too shaped by our fears of getting old. We say middle-aged and old-aged, but we never say young-aged. We love the word *youthful*, but we will never hear anyone joyously called middleful or oldful. We are known as teenaged for a brief time in our lives, and then we get to be young adults. After that, we are simply aging.

In modern, youth-oriented cultures, the word *aging* carries negative associations, so we do not refer to turning twenty-one or thirty as aging; we call that growing up. We use *aging* only in connection with people over forty. Although we may love wine and cheese that have aged well, we do not seem to appreciate or respect that process in women as we get older. In a culture that fears growing old, we assume that once we pass forty, we will lose our strength, beauty, and vitality.

The words we use matter. They consciously and unconsciously affect our attitudes and feelings about ourselves and others. For instance, calling someone a child is very different from calling someone childish. One word simply describes a life stage, while the other negatively describes a person's behavior. In the same way, the shift from middle-*aged* to *Middle*hood may seem small, but its implications are immense. When we put the emphasis on *middle*, our questions begin to change. Less often will we ask the questions of youth: "Who am I? What is my purpose in life?" Now the central question is, "What does it mean to be in the middle of my life?" More questions flow from that one: "Am I being true to myself? What else do I need or want to do?" The simple change to the broader term *Middlehood* elicits more creative possibilities for exploring the challenges, joys, and complexities of this time.

If we think of life as climbing a mountain, then Middlehood begins at the halfway point on its upward trail. We have spent all of our years prior to this time gathering experiences, knowledge, and skills. We have fulfilled early dreams and built relationships— and we may have accumulated some regrets. Right now, we have access to everything from our past, and every bit of it brings us here, to the present. But we are not done yet, not by a long shot; we also have a future: new dreams, loves, accomplishments, failures, and discoveries waiting to be explored. We are right in the middle and can look with equal ability and enthusiasm in both directions. We are full of rich memories and past experiences, and we have exciting plans waiting to unfold. We can claim ignorance and authority, wisdom and naiveté. We can welcome people of all ages as friends and see the value of their stories and experiences. What a potent and exciting place to be!

There is real power and richness in this time, but in order to find that treasure, we must be willing to turn the page into a new chapter of our lives. This part of the process is where we often get stuck. What is required is releasing our past, our youth, and finding our way through confusion and challenges to our new place, our Middlehood.

In some ways, this time is reminiscent of the passage we made as teens: our bodies are doing strange and unexpected things, and our emotions refuse to be organized and contained. We feel buffeted and chaotic. In other ways, it is very different than our coming of age as adults. At eighteen, we could not wait to finish the metamorphosis into our adult selves. But now we drag our feet, not at all sure that we want to go through the doorway into the next room.

We know that we are getting older; we can feel the changes happening. Sometimes, entering Middlehood feels like an evolutionary change, a natural progression through the days and years that make up our lives. Other times, it is as stunning as a revolution, the complete overthrow of life as we have known it. Whether it sneaks up on us or is a dawning realization, we may lose our sense of "normal" and worry about whether we will ever find it again. Maybe most discouraging is the dreadful feeling that something is inexorably dragging us along without our permission. "Stop, stop!" we want to say. "I can't get old; I'm not ready yet!"

I don't think about being fifty-three years old until it is kind of waved in my face. So I think I would definitely lean more toward the word Middlehood because, frankly, my brain thinks I'm still fourteen years old.

> ~ Kathy J., 53-year-old

The years from forty to sixty-five are full of change, and truthfully, none of us escape the rigors of the middle phase of life. This is not a movie, and most of us are not getting age-defying face-lifts. Emotional changes occur along with physical ones. Middlehood women are tired, forgetful, and easily frustrated. We are grieving and confused and afraid. We have put on weight, don't sleep well, and have weird aches and pains. But, despite these challenges, to be open to the new insights of Middlehood is to accept this evolutionary process and to be willing to explore what is good, rich, enhancing, empowering, and exciting about this time in our lives. We may find that we have deeper, more honest relationships; new kinds of creativity, energy, and passion; a wonderful sense of humor; and the beginnings of true wisdom about how life really works. This time can be most extraordinary.

What is best about this time? I look the best. I am the most self-confident I have ever been. I can tell the difference between people lying to me, conning me, and guilt-tripping me. I have a resonance in my heart with Truth and Wisdom that I trust. I don't have to struggle to feel good about myself.

> ~ Rhea M., 58-year-old

For all my complaints and fretting, I would never want to go back to my younger days. . . . I live daily with a sense of inner security and rootedness that utterly evaded me in my youth.

> ~ Cindy L., 49-year-old

In order to let ourselves expand from fear and frustration into the fullness of Middlehood possibilities, we must do the work of starting a new chapter in our lives. This is hard work and there is no straight line to it. We go up and down, around and around, learning, forgetting, stretching out, and shrinking back. Some days we are full of hope and energy, itching to take it all on; other times, not so much. But ready or not, here it comes—"The Change" is upon us.

Let's take a look at some of the feelings and growing insights of Middlehood. In the left-hand column are feelings that many of us know all too well. Most of us will be afraid, overwhelmed, and exhausted sometimes. When those feelings lose their fluidity and become rigid, we are going to feel stuck, depressed, or hopeless. On the right are the same qualities and insights that can evolve into a new stage of life awareness and attitude. In a sense, the right-hand column holds the remedies for the struggles and concerns of the left-hand one. Look at the powerful shift we can make when we let our limiting feelings evolve into a new self-concept.

Feelings	Evolving Insights
We are afraid—a lot—of death, loss, illness, loneliness, and poverty.	We are afraid but very brave. We are resourceful and try new things; make new friends; take steps to prevent potential problems that we actually have control over; and learn to accept what we do not have control over.
We get depressed/ immobilized.	We are sometimes sad, but we learn to find strategies and resources for coping. We keep our sense of humor and do things to strengthen our sense of hope and purpose. We are not afraid to ask for help from others.

Feelings	Evolving Insights
We feel invisible, left out, and overlooked.	We value our experience, even if others do not seem to. We spend time with people who respect and appreciate us. We make a commitment to see and speak to others even if they do not see us. We learn to communicate more creatively.
We feel achy, fat, and unattractive.	We take steps to improve our physical well-being and health. We focus more on our energy and less on trying to look younger. We accept our changes and new limitations by trying new activities.
We forget things—words, names, details—which increases our feelings of frustration and loss of trust in ourselves.	We are not embarrassed to write things down! We also find a resurgence of older memories reminding us of people and experiences that still carry important and valuable lessons. We trust our intuition more.
We feel ourselves grieving our many losses: parents, family members, friends, youth, beauty, and strength.	We are willing to let go of the past as it was. We cherish memories and are full of gratitude for all of our relationships and loved ones, past and present. We stop looking at younger people as models for what is beautiful and strong.
We feel tired and weaker.	We build our energy with positive things. We develop new kinds of strength, try different activities and hobbies, and find ourselves powerful in new ways. We learn to plan for the places and circumstances where we are not strong.

Feelings	Evolving Insights
We feel a disconnect between how we look on the outside and how we feel on the inside.	We really do know ourselves and are much more honest with ourselves and others. There is more consistency between how we act and how we feel. We are still surprised by our physical changes but are able to accept them and adapt as needed.
We may be in relationships that do not feel satisfying or fulfilling, but we are afraid to do anything about it.	We know our most important and long-lasting relationship is with ourselves. We are willing to do the work necessary to keep relationships growing, but we would rather be alone than in a relationship that is harmful or limiting.
We feel powerless and at the mercy of outside forces.	We begin to assume our authority based on our lives, experience, and knowledge, and are willing to be teachers. We know what we know, and we are able to call on that accumulated wisdom.
We feel lost and confused. We have lost our sense of purpose and fear we have nothing to look forward to.	We can get to our core needs and feelings quickly. We let go of fluff, shoulds, and oughts. We are open to new ideas and people, develop new dreams and goals. We can refocus/reframe. We achieve clarity about our life's purpose.

The left-hand column is mostly about what we are struggling with or fear we are losing. The right-hand column shows a willingness to accept things as they are and to take action to move into a new perspective or activities. When we focus too much on what is decreasing or disappearing in our lives, we forget to see what is growing larger and stronger.

I'm not as strong as I used to be, and I have to carry my compost in smaller buckets, but after all these years of gardening, I sure know what to do to help my flowers grow!

~ 65-year-old

This is the best time of my life. I like being centered; knowing that I love me and I am lovable. Feeling calm and patient with what is around me; having the wisdom of experience through which to assess events and the compassion of spiritual practice to engage in the world.

~ Susan McK., 63-year-old

At forty, we are just stepping into a phase of life that stretches more than twenty years into the future. We are not over the hill and on our way down; Middlehood is almost one third of our lives! The best is *not* all behind us. Of course we face challenges and changes; there are always challenges and changes, no matter how old we are. There is no stopping the changes or going back, and here in Middlehood, we begin to understand this with a depth we have never known.

There are no universal answers to the question, "What does it mean to be in the middle of my life?" Instead, we explore, looking for meaning in all the changes in our lives. We can focus less on the negative aspects of aging and make a realistic assessment of where we are, not a fearful one. We can walk through Middlehood with our eyes wide open, full of curiosity, hope, and courage.

Why Middlehood? We need a larger concept of this life stage that provides richer and fuller possibilities. Are we really becoming more limited? Maybe so, in some ways, but we are becoming more powerful in many new ways. Most of us do not realize this until we are solidly into our Middlehood, when it dawns on us that some things are better than they have ever been.

CHAPTER 2

Women and Mountains I

The outer path we take is public knowledge, but the path with heart is an inner one. The two come together when who we are that is seen in the world coincides with who we deeply are. As we grow wiser, we become aware that the important forks in the road are usually not about choices that will show up on any public record; they are decisions and struggles to do with choosing love or fear; anger or forgiveness; pride or humility. They are soul-shaping choices.

~ Jean Shinoda Bolen, *Crones Don't Whine: Concentrated Wisdom for Juicy Women*

When you stand and share your story in an empowering way, your story will heal you and your story will heal somebody else.

~ Iyanla Vanzant

THE IMAGE OF LIFE AS A mountain is familiar to people all over the world. Many spiritual traditions use this image to teach young people how to grow in strength, courage, and grace. People who climb mountains and live in mountains understand the rigors and exhilaration of making a trek to a high place and marveling at the view. Climbers or not, we can understand the beauty and power and mystery of those seemingly remote places that are easy to see but hard to attain. Not all of us climb physical mountains, but we climb real mountains made of our years, our joys, and our accomplishments. They are also made of challenges and obstacles we face, whether fears, poverty, disabilities, or other people's expectations. Over and over in our lives, we will struggle and climb to reach a peak, only to find more and higher peaks beyond what we were able to imagine from below.

The true stories of how women have climbed their mountains are inspiring and educational for all of us. As we listen to women's stories about their lives and adventures, we find enormous truths in these personal tales. Strangers become companions on our journeys.

———

To the Roof of Africa by Jane Treat

Some years ago, I heard Reneé O'Connor tell the story of her climb up Mount Kilimanjaro. This personal story of accomplishment is also a story containing classic images of some of life's most profound themes. The world's myths and spiritual literature are full of such stories—a young person heads off for fun and adventure, and ends up on a true quest for wisdom, power, and vision. This is a story we all know; it calls to us, waking memories of a time when we were young and dreamed of adventure. Although we are not young anymore, inside each of us is still a brave and strong woman who has reached down deep and found the determination to face her fears and overcome obstacles.

Part One: Reneé's Story

*Reneé, in her midtwenties, and her mother, Sandra
Wilson, in her late forties, had planned the vacation of
a lifetime. Africa! After a visit to Egypt, they traveled to
northeast Tanzania to climb Mount Kilimanjaro, the
highest mountain in all of Africa—19,340 feet. Mount
Kilimanjaro is so high that, although only three degrees
from the equator, its snow-covered summit is often lost in
the clouds.*

*Amazingly, it is not necessary to be a technical climber to
go up Mount Kilimanjaro. But all hikers must contend with
a debilitating, potentially serious or even fatal condition
known as acute mountain sickness (altitude sickness).
Altitude sensitivity is unpredictable in individuals, and
physical fitness and age are not the deciding factors.
Although Reneé was strong and fit, she was allergic to the
medicine that many hikers take to alleviate the effects of
altitude sickness.*

*Undaunted, Sandra and Reneé joined their group and
began the trek up the mountain. From the trailhead at
Marangu Gate, they followed the gentle paths of the lower
levels of Mount Kilimanjaro, slowly winding their way
through lush tropical forest as they hiked the first few
thousand feet. The beginning of the hike was easy, more a
walk than a climb, and yet, "Pole, pole (pole-ay, pole-ay),"
the guides admonished even at this early stage, "slowly,
slowly." After a few short hours, they reached Mandara
Hut at nine thousand feet for their first night on Mount
Kilimanjaro.*

*On the way to Horombo Hut for the second night, the hikers
ascended to more than twelve thousand feet. They left the
canopy of the lower slopes as the trail broke free of the trees
and led on through meadows and moorland. Above ten
thousand feet, most people begin to react to the decreased*

oxygen. *Once the headaches and fatigue began, Reneé and Sandra could no longer depend on physical strength alone. From that point on, will power and determination were also necessary to keep them moving up the mountain.*

Far above the plains that surround Mount Kilimanjaro, and then beyond the forests and meadows of the lower levels, the mountain turns to rock and sand. Growing weaker and slower, and no longer able to eat, Sandra and Reneé forged on through the biting wind and barren rock towards the great dome of Kibo and the summit at Uhuru (Freedom) Peak.

Shortly after midnight on the fourth day, they left Kibo Hut and began the final torturous ascent. It was important to reach the top of Mount Kilimanjaro early in the day before the gale force winds that buffet the summit became too dangerous. Pole, pole, they struggled through the mountain darkness, zigzagging up the steep and treacherous gravel path, falling farther and farther behind the others in the group. Higher up the mountain, the lights of their fellow travelers showed them the way, marking the switchback trail for them to follow.

Just below Gilman's Point on the rim of the ancient volcano, Sandra was seized by a severe attack of altitude sickness. Confused and disoriented, she became violently ill and shook uncontrollably. Clearly, she could go no farther, and her only remedy was to descend as quickly as possible. Alarmed by her mother's condition, Reneé wanted to take Sandra down. But Sandra was adamant: "This is as far as I go, Reneé, but you go on. Go all the way if you can."

Leaving her mother in the care of a guide, Reneé trudged on. She found a simple rhythm to carry her—take a step and breathe, take another step and breathe again. Pole, pole—one step, one breath. Stumbling and weak, each movement a monumental effort, Reneé inched her way along the rocky trail. Behind her lay the thousands of steps she had taken to get to this point. Behind her, she hoped, her mother was waiting, recovering in the lower altitude. Ahead of her was the roof of Africa, if she could only make it. One step at a time through scree and snow; one step at a time along the rim of the crater; pole, pole. Each step nearly impossible; take a step and breathe. Each step one step closer to the top; take a step and breathe.

Finally, nauseated and exhausted, the last of the group to arrive, Reneé staggered the final few feet to the pinnacle of Mount Kilimanjaro. She had made it and stood, for a moment, at the top of Africa. Then she collapsed. But there was little time to rest—the winds were rising, and it was dangerous to remain exposed on the summit. She mustered the strength to shakily write her name in the book that is kept at Uhuru Peak, and then the group began the journey down, heading back towards air and strength, family and home.

———

From the moment I heard Reneé's account, I loved her story and marveled at the strength and determination that got her to the top of Mount Kilimanjaro. But I also wondered about Sandra's story. What did the climb mean to Sandra? What did it feel like to have to stop so close to the peak? What allowed her to send her daughter on without her?

Like Sandra, we are still on our quest for wisdom and have not only determination but also years of experience to help us understand our fears and know our limitations. Not many myths or stories offer guidance for this time in our lives, so we often must write the story ourselves. As with Reneé and Sandra, the external terrain may look the same, but the inner journey will always reflect the challenges and insights of our own perspective and experience.

Part Two: Sandra's Story in Her Own Words

When Reneé asked me to go to Africa, I felt a sense of numbing disbelief that an opportunity of this size was indeed reality. To climb Mount Kilimanjaro, as with everything that we choose to conquer, would bring learning. Sometimes we get only one chance, and some things cannot be rushed.

It is extremely difficult to move in high altitude because the oxygen is so thin, plus there is the freezing cold, gravel, and uphill slant. Reneé was right behind me the whole way and kept reminding me to go slowly, "pole, pole." At one point I told her that I was really tired, and she said, "Take a step, take a breath." I found that when our strength is gone, we have an internal will that can take us further.

Stopping at Gilman's Point was a mixed blessing. I looked up at Uhuru Peak, which looked like it was only a relatively short climb away. In reality, it was 960 feet! It appeared to be straight up gravel, and I couldn't imagine how I would be able to make it. Part of me was relieved that I could let myself stop. Still, I was so close. But there was no way I could get there. I was exhausted, stricken with altitude sickness, and I knew I needed some strength to get myself back down to a lower elevation, and there was no time to rest.

Reneé was ready to take me down, and we were running out of time. It was now or never. Just then a guide told me that he would go with Reneé to the peak and return. Another guide offered to go down with me. That was all that I needed to hear. The decision was made; Reneé would go on without me.

We live our lives so fast, we can easily miss important milestones. Africa represents a rite of passage for Reneé and the end of a chapter for me. We had our time together, and now it was time for Reneé to go on with her life.

For me, not getting to Uhuru Peak helped me to realize that some things were not meant for me to achieve. It helped me to appreciate my gifts and develop them. The climb also taught me to accept my limitations, hopefully with grace (meaning no whining)!

————

Life as a mountain—we all know that image. Those of us in the middle years of our lives, like Sandra, know that we do not peak the mountain in our youth and then spend the rest of our lives on a downhill slide into old age and death. Rather, we spend our whole lives climbing our mountains, and our experience teaches us, as Sandra discovered, that not all peaks are ours, and sometimes an insurmountable obstacle means it is time to change direction.

When we are young, we often begin our mountains as Reneé did—with enthusiasm and nervousness, believing ourselves capable of all things if only we work hard enough. Then life happens: boulders block our trails, scree makes it hard to keep our footing, and sometimes storms blow up, and we are injured or lose our way. Amazingly, sometimes our successes alter our climb, and sometimes seeming failures provide our richest opportunities for learning and achieving. Whatever the challenges, it is guaranteed that none of us will climb straight up our mountains with no obstacles or detours along the way.

So where are we on the trail? Where is Middlehood? It is a critical, crucial time that begins somewhere in the middle of our lives, and it is only part way up the mountain. We have already done plenty of zigging and zagging up our trails, and sometimes we are tired. But we are still climbing. We still have spirit and determination, and we have also achieved an astonishing view. Halfway up the mountain is where we can begin to see the awesome line of lights that leads us on and the gorgeous line of lights that follows.

Another gift of our time on the trail is that we look around and see unexpected people traveling with us. We all start at the base of the mountain in our different places, where circumstances and life began for us. In our youth, we followed the seemingly separate paths described by our various languages, cultures, religions, habits, and economics. These unique circumstances must not be minimized, because they have colored and flavored who we are today.

As we live and climb further up the mountain, disparate paths begin to merge. Perhaps we are intrigued by the gifts of other cultures and find harmony and connection to people from another part of the world. Maybe we love technology and are surprised at how easy it is to find camaraderie with young people who love it too. Whatever we find along the way, there are still many paths— but maybe they are more connected now. The diversity of our circumstances fades, and the commonality of our journeys and our deeper similarities emerge. The higher we get up the mountain, the more we find shared experiences. Our lives are still unique, but we are not alone; other travelers become our companions.

In the images that Sandra and Reneé describe, we see that life is the mountain—beautiful, torturous, surprising, and challenging. The comparisons go on and on. Most of us will not climb Mount Kilimanjaro, but we already climb our own rocky trails through struggle and pain, failure and success. We follow the lights of the ones who have gone before us, and we walk on after our parents have stopped. Sometimes we stride, other times we stagger, and occasionally we collapse. And perhaps we find that humility is the truest response to our greatest victories. After all, life, like Mount Kilimanjaro, takes everything we have.

Maybe the lesson for how to live is the same as how to climb mountains: take a step and breathe, and keep on climbing.

Reflection Questions

- How would I describe the mountain that I have been climbing?
- In what ways have my paths changed over time?
- What obstacles have I encountered? Were they dead ends? If so, what happened when I changed direction? If not, how did I overcome them?

CHAPTER 3

The Equation for Transformation: Making Transitions

Courage doesn't always roar. Sometimes, courage is the quiet voice at the end of the day, saying, "I will try again tomorrow." It takes courage to change your style, your opinion, the path you walk, your hat! It takes courage to let go of the weighty parts of your past. It takes courage to find your own voice.

~ Mary Anne Radmacher, *Courage Doesn't Always Roar*

MOST OF US HAVE PLENTY OF experience with change in our lives. Sometimes, the changes come naturally, one choice leading to another in an orderly fashion, and we can take one step at a time. Sometimes, we can even see where we are going. Other times, change comes abruptly, joltingly in a flash, and we are left in shambles, putting our lives back together after a storm we did not expect or want.

In 2010, we had a major earthquake here in Christchurch, New Zealand. It was a catastrophic and life-changing event in which we lost our home of twenty-eight years, a place full of memories and love. We also lost our perspective in

19

life. Our fears at this time were all-consuming. Money was irrelevant because we were unable to purchase anything at all, but support, no matter how small or insignificant to the giver, was magnified by the receiver. This we took with us every day as we wandered through this most difficult time. We found that a touch, a word, or a hug meant everything to us and those we encountered along the way. Family, humanity, neighbors, and the entire community shared, supplied, and supported each other as we planned our rebuilding process. In 2013, we finally began to rebuild our home in another place. Now, as we look to the future, we see, touch, and feel in a whole different way. We look at life as a whole, not as a day or an event. We love deeply and look at love far beyond the physical. We have grown in so many ways, and now our tears merge through life, love, laughter, and that rainbow called the future.

~ Yvonne McB., 60-year-old

Yvonne's life was turned upside down in a traumatic way. Most of us will not lose everything so literally, but we will all go through times when we feel like we have to start completely over.

And then there are less dramatic times, when we have found ourselves trapped or stuck in situations, and we really *need* a change. We have changed jobs, moved to new places, even broken up long-term relationships in an effort to start a new chapter in our lives. Each of those moves made a difference, but maybe not the profound change we were hoping to find. Likely, we just took our baggage with us. We found another partner or spouse with the same issues as the one we left, or discovered ourselves stuck in the same way in the new job.

So what does it take to make a real change or transition in our lives? How do we know when we are ready, and how can we make that transition in a positive way? There is not much guidance out there to help us negotiate a real passage. Whenever we make a transition in our lives, we are beginning something new, but *how* we do it—that is the secret.

Our society believes that we must remove ourselves from the old place as quickly as possible and jump full force into whatever we have chosen as our new place. We try to fix everything that way, from relationships to weight problems. Using that method, we miss something along the way: finishing things, seeing things through, and bringing them to completion with time for understanding and reflection.

To really make a change, any change, we must let go of what has been and trust that the truth of who we are will come through in a new way. No matter what we are ending—old fears, old beliefs, past relationships, or past images of ourselves—the process is essentially the same. Even healing requires an ending of sorts. To truly heal, we must be willing to change.

My whole regeneration of me is to focus on the things that I love and the things that make me an interested participant in life instead of going along and reacting.

~ Sharon T., 48-year-old

Teachers and coauthors Meredith Little and Steven Foster created a valuable tool for orienting and navigating the inevitable changes in life: the Equation for Transformation. Simple in concept, it is challenging to implement because society teaches us the exact opposite. The Equation for Transformation teaches us to:

Start with an ending.
Go into the middle.
Pass through to a new beginning.

So what does this mean in terms of our real lives? What needs to end? How do we do that? What happens in the middle? How in the world does a new beginning come about?

Let us start with the first piece: endings, a strange place to begin a new phase in our lives. But for many of us in Middlehood, it feels like nearly everything *is* ending, as though the world as we have known it is disappearing. We feel whole sections of our lives slipping away or changing without our permission. We have deep feelings of loss for the end of our youth. Our physical strength and beauty are waning. Images of ourselves blur and become confused. Who we are on the inside and how we look on the outside no longer coincide. Our children are grown or nearly so, and moving away. Our lighthearted hopes for the future are fading. Our ability to "live for today" because we have plenty of time to "settle down and get serious" seems immature, even silly. "I will do that next year" gives us pause—will we really? And stunningly, people are dying—parents, spouses, partners, and friends. Suddenly, we realize that we are running out of time. There is more urgency, less of a relaxed sense of taking life as it comes. Now we must hurry—to fulfill our dreams, save money for retirement, write that book, or get in shape. We have to make things happen—NOW! SOON!

We have become afraid. Looming over us are fears of:

- Getting old: becoming incapacitated, limited, or sick
- Death: our own, our parents, spouses/partners, siblings, extended family, friends; and the less tangible deaths: a way of life, a dream, or an image of ourselves
- Uselessness or even worse, being a burden to others
- Loss of purpose through empty nest or retirement

Is that all we can look forward to? Must we have face-lifts, affairs, or breakdowns to negotiate this time? Of course not—those so-called solutions are part of the false picture of what it means to be women in our middle years. Yes, fear and grief have become visible threads in the lives we weave, but we are so much more than that, and we *know* it, regardless of what popular culture says.

So how can starting with endings help us hold the many conflicting and tumultuous feelings of this time? First, let us look at the ideas of evolution and revolution. From *Merriam-Webster's Collegiate Dictionary (11ᵗʰ edition)*, the word *evolution* means "a process of continuous change from a lower, simpler, or worse to a higher, more complex, or better state: growth." *Revolution* means "a sudden, radical, or complete change"; or "a fundamental change in the way of thinking about or visualizing something: a change of paradigm."

So which is it? Maybe it is both. Evolutionary change is slow enough that we can see ourselves changing only when we look back over time. We can say, "Oh, I used to feel that way, but I guess I don't anymore." Revolutionary change occurs when what previously felt normal is suddenly altered. For instance, it may be seem inconsequential, but, a woman who has been a night person all her life will be disconcerted to suddenly find herself nodding off on the couch at 7:30 p.m. and then waking up—being wide awake—at 2:00 a.m.

We experienced evolutionary change when we grew from children into adults. Our bodies changed, and so did our ideas and feelings. The change was gradual, slow and steady, and we did not notice much on a day-to-day basis. The process felt natural, and we carried a sense of hope about what the changes from growing older would bring. Every so often, as teens, something would make us pause and look back. An aunt we had not seen in a long time would look surprised and say, "Wow, you've gotten so tall!" We realized that this aunt who used to carry us piggyback was now much shorter—way too small to carry us.

As we became adults and headed towards thirty, we noticed small changes. Maybe our skin seemed drier, and we no longer got pimples as often. That was a good thing! Maybe we could still push our bodies to extremes by staying up all night or spending a weekend playing strenuous sports, but we paid a price: sore muscles or a cold. Perhaps we suddenly developed allergies. We noticed all of these changes and absorbed them without much concern. "Ah well," we thought, "guess I'm not a kid anymore."

On we went through our thirties, raising our kids, getting better at our work, shifting up and down with the waves of what life brought us. We did not think of ourselves as aging exactly. We thought of ourselves as growing: settling into ourselves, finding our place and purpose in life. We were confident that we still had plenty of time to find the right person, have a baby, go back to school, or get the dream job we wanted.

Then forty looms, and all kinds of things start to happen. The change does not feel evolutionary anymore; suddenly, revolution is upon us. Physical changes accelerate. Now we are asking questions like:

- Why can't I see clearly anymore?
- Am I too old to have a child?
- Why can't I get rid of these five extra pounds?

Those changes feel sudden, but of course, they are not. They have been developing for a long time, but they seem to suddenly appear, and we may be shocked. For many women in our late thirties and early forties, that sense of shock includes a feeling of dread about what is coming. Suddenly, time is no longer our friend. Now time begins to push us.

Emotionally, we begin to take stock of ourselves, measuring and evaluating. Are we happy in our relationship? Are we alone and feeling like we are running out of time? Have we achieved what we wanted, or are we falling behind on the goals we set? We realize it is no longer possible to be precocious or "mature for our age." We are not "up and coming" anymore. Those descriptions are for young people, no longer for us. We are simply wherever we are: happy and fulfilled, lost and frustrated, or somewhere in between. Now as we meet the big 4-0 and beyond, everything is suddenly about aging and no longer about growing.

As a culture, we have a terrible time with aging, seeing it as inevitable steps towards death. We do everything we can to hide it, avoid it, postpone it. When we come to a time of transition, like turning forty or sixty-five, we resist or we are just plain lost and have no clue what to do. We respond to backhanded compliments like, "Wow, you sure don't look fifty," with a mixture of pleasure and confusion. "What am I supposed to look like?" Should we step into denial and hope that no one notices the new wrinkles or thicker waist? Should we just fade into invisibility with a sense of defeat? We see that reaction in ourselves and certainly in the popular culture around us.

Once we are solidly in our Middlehood, issues of aging become everyday topics of conversation: menopause, memory blips, peculiar things appearing on our skin, colonoscopies, and mammograms. We start watching the stock market and worry about our IRAs and 401(k)s. We get out calendars and calculators, trying to figure out when we can really afford to retire.

But something else also begins to happen. We notice more subtle changes. Some of them are even kind of encouraging! We notice that it is easier to say no to things we really do not want. And amazingly, we are much clearer about what we do want. We feel a deepening sense of being comfortable with ourselves, less confusion about who we really are, and more confidence about what we know. Maybe, just maybe, it is not all bad.

I find that the older I get, the less patience I have for some things that other people are doing. I have to bite my tongue, because I'm going to tell somebody off someday! I have no patience for waiting in long lines and certainly no patience for waiting on hold for anybody or anything. I have to restrain myself because I'll just go up and tell them. I find that I'm much more out there—even with my language.

~ Carol S., 50-year-old

So what can we do to stop the chaotic forward-backward movement and take our steps more confidently? How can we quiet the voice in us that keeps saying, "What is wrong with me?" In our heads, we know there is nothing wrong, but we also know we are going through a big change that requires a lot of work.

How can we help this process happen?

Start with an Ending

When we begin the Equation for Transformation, most of us arrive dragging suitcases and old trunks and duffle bags full of stuff: the baggage we have collected for decades. Much of that stuff is clutter, out-of-date clothes that no longer fit, half-done projects we do not even care about finishing, guilt and regrets for things that no one else even remembers. Hauling all that unsorted stuff is hard and takes a huge amount of time and energy.

What helps is to turn around and lovingly put our arms around all of our past. Not every woman wants to do the work involved in this part of the process. It can stir up feelings of sadness and pain, but the purpose is to free ourselves from all that clutter and baggage from the past. Hidden in the midst of the jumble are treasures that hold the real value and gifts of our lives. But in order to unearth those precious pieces of gold and make a real change, we must let go of what has been and trust that what is true and important will come through.

Here are some practical strategies that will help us complete the ending step of the Equation for Transformation and prepare us to take on the middle step. We can choose any that feel right or add others that are more personal.

- Clean—closets, attic, basement, garage, old garden beds, filing cabinets, whatever feels right.
- Give away all extraneous stuff—pare down, lighten the load, let go of stuff.
- Pay debts.
- Return borrowed things.
- Make amends—phone, write, visit, whatever. Say the words; communicate regrets for anything we have not handled well. For everyone we cannot directly apologize to, do something in their honor to indicate our good intentions. Fix everything that can be fixed, then bless the rest and let it go.
- Express gratitude to family, friends, mentors, heroes. Be very specific; do not use vague statements like, "Thanks for being my friend." Tell people what they have meant to you and why you have valued them. Most people are astonished and hugely embarrassed to be told these things. Persevere—despite their self-consciousness, *everyone* needs to know that they have meant something to someone.
- Look at pictures from your past. Acknowledge what has ended and get in touch with what is still alive in you.
- Make a will or trust, or at the very least, a list of your possessions that you would like to pass on.
- Make a list of your regrets. Do something about as many of them as you can. Make this list as short as possible.
- Make a list of all the things you wanted to do and decide if you still want to do them.

· Make a gratitude list and identify moments of joy. Make this list as long as possible and keep adding to it.

The point of these activities is to make peace with our past. Go ahead and remember. There will be laughter and sadness as we go through old photos and boxes and drawers. Perhaps looking at pictures of ourselves as children will remind us of something we have forgotten. Maybe reviving an old friendship will bring us a new ally at this time in our lives. We can lovingly keep everything we really value, whether keepsakes, friendships, or dreams. The easiest way to honor our past and move forward is to find our gratitude.

The end of a twenty-seven-year-marriage in my fifties, through a contentious seven-year process in the courts, made letting go of that life both an agony and a relief. During those tumultuous years, I was diagnosed with endometrial cancer that was over with a quick-fix hysterectomy, and I was back to my plan for life after divorce. A routine mammogram, ten years later, revealed breast cancer, with another easy fix—lumpectomy and radiation. This time, however, I did not return to my life plan. Instead, within two months following my breast cancer diagnosis, I sold my house in one state and bought one in another state to be near family and live more freely and spontaneously. Starting over in my sixties felt somewhat like the new beginnings and opportunities that I experienced in my late teens going off to college. How much easier it has been now, with the wisdom of age and the courage to let go of the familiar and comfortable life that I learned you cannot really plan. With confidence and faith, I am embracing the new adventures, love, joy, and laughter that each day brings.

~ Ann C., 62-year-old

We may need to forgive ourselves and others. Whatever we can do will help us let go of all that ties us to our past limitations and fears. No longer letting the past define us is a step towards the freedom we need to move fully into the present. Remember that this clearing process is as much for sorting through old ideas and beliefs as for any emotional or material clutter. When seeking wisdom and the connections between our past and future, we must be willing to face this review process. If we wish for a new, true vision to sustain us, we must find and let go of the old beliefs that are now too small.

We have sorted and packed our most valuable possessions and our truest beliefs into a manageable backpack and suitcase, consciously ending a phase of life. So now what happens? What we have done is create space, both physical and spiritual, for new things to appear. In the empty space we have made, we will discover new energy and hope. Our youth may be over, but our lives are certainly not. We still have years, decades of life to plan and live. So let us blow a kiss to our youthful selves and find out what we want to do now.

Go into the Middle

After all the activity and work of doing endings, most of us will come to a quiet place. It may not be apparent on the outside, but inside we feel an urge to pull in or pull back from everything that demands our attention. This desire to be more internally focused is complicated, because our external lives do not stop. We are in demand everywhere—family, work, and responsibilities of every kind.

At this point, we can look for tools that help us create the time and space to be quiet. Many of us find that turning to spiritual practices, such as prayer and meditation, will help. Others will find peace in nature, music, art, long walks, yoga, or talking with friends over coffee. Whatever our method, it is important that we make and take the time to listen to ourselves.

After working at full-time jobs all my life, I made a big decision to work for myself. I incorporated my business, put together long-term business plans, and lined up short-term jobs. I left behind a regular salary, full benefits, and the comfortable feeling of knowing when the next paycheck was coming. Unfortunately, things did not work out as I had planned. Then came all the worries: panic attacks about how to pay the mortgage and bills; doubts about whether I did the right thing; and the anxious feeling of not being someone who goes to a job every day and just plays on weekends. I have never experienced not knowing what to do and the insecurity that goes with that. It was difficult to change the way I saw myself. I talked long and hard to my friends and partner. I did relaxing activities to relieve the stress, and I realized that I needed to be kind and patient with myself. In time, I realized that my early plans were too small, so my partner and I changed directions and launched into new and exciting possibilities together.

~ 56-year-old

But this part can be hard because we have conflicting feelings about being still. In some ways, this stage is the hardest for modern people. We feel guilty when we are not doing anything, as if we are wasting time. So we do all the work of the first step and then we... wait. We really hate that. Like being midway through a tunnel, we feel tempted to turn back. We do not really want to, but the end is not in sight, and we are impatient, frustrated, and desperate for something to happen. This is the dark place of waiting, and we begin to worry. Have we made a mistake? Is it too late? Are we crazy to think we can change at this point in our lives? What is going to happen?

This in-between place, the pause between the old and the new, is where we must trust and be patient. Why do we have to sit and wait? Because it takes time to digest all that is in us, to let ideas simmer and brew. To let that happen, we must stay in the present, not dwell on the past or try to impose an old idea on the future. Distracting ourselves with busy activities or unhealthy habits is tempting. Instead, the challenge is to be creative and find ways to fill our moments and days with healthy, joyful choices. Our day-to-day lives will continue to demand our attention and energy, so we will have to find ways to balance those activities and the reflective time we may anxiously desire.

What can we do while we wait in the middle step? How can we make this stage positive and constructive rather than torturous? Here are some suggestions for completing this stage of the Equation for Transformation and preparing for new beginnings. As always, we can choose any that feel right or add others that are more personal.

- Breathe—deeply and consciously.
- Sleep or rest as much as you can.
- Walk, exercise, and eat well. Attend to what your body tells you.
- Relax when you sense that you want to force things to happen.
- Talk to friends and family about fears, hopes, and dreams.
- Fill your present moments with love, beauty, and kindness for yourself and others.
- Enjoy movies, books, and music that lift your spirits and inspire you.
- Take your focus off your worries through prayer, meditation, or healthy activities.
- Notice what catches your attention. What makes you laugh? Or cry? Or intrigues you?

The easiest way to remember that we need trust is to think of a seed. We plant a seed and then we wait. The miracles of life and growth are all happening under the surface where we cannot see them. If we anxiously dig up the seed to see what is going on, we will kill it, abort the process, and prevent the natural cycle from happening. Remember to trust in this: the dark places where we plant seeds are also fertile places. For instance, the ancient Indo-Europeans considered black the color of life and power because they understood that all things are born from waiting in the dark. What we have planted will become visible, but that is not the beginning of the process—it is only the revolutionary appearance of something new. The key is to stay present and keep the door to hope open.

Pass Through to a New Beginning

And somehow miracles happen. We move from the dark, inner place of waiting into the light: a baby is born, a seed sprouts, or a new idea comes to life. There is real mystery here. How? When? What changed? We have no easy answers to these questions. Does a new idea come as a bolt of lightning or the gradual graying of the dark? Does it evolve slowly or bloom overnight as we sleep? Did a word from a friend suddenly have new meaning, or was it a favorite passage from a long-loved book or an old favorite song?

What does a new beginning mean to each of us? It could be tangible, like a new job or a new relationship, but it could also be finding ourselves with a new attitude or ready for a new way of life. We could find ourselves feeling lighter, less encumbered or, conversely, more deeply rooted and involved in something we care about passionately. This complexity makes the work of the Equation for Transformation a rich, unique journey for each of us. The possibilities for Middlehood women are many and varied, but if we honor the truth of who we are and have done the work of clearing away extraneous clutter, we will find a choice that is appropriate to each of us.

Remember the inklings we got when we accepted that we were now in the middle of our lives? We may find that those inklings are solidifying into a new realization: we have never been better in our lives! Despite the challenges and physical changes, when we look at how we feel inside, we discover that we are not broken or sinking into oblivion. No matter what society says or thinks about Middlehood women, we are strong, passionate, effective, and clear about who we are and what we can do.

My husband left me and my three kids seven years ago. I remember how angry he was and how he said to me, "You should sell the house and give me half of it, because you are not going to make it without me." I told myself I was going to make it no matter what. I'm so lucky to have three kids to go home to, working seven days a week, saving a little here and a little there to keep the roof over our heads and put my daughter through college and my son through barber school. Three years later, after my divorce, I paid off my car and then asked for a loan to start my own business. It was hard in the beginning, with the economy so bad, but my business partner and I made it through the first two years building new clients. Not a day goes by that I don't thank God for everything. Owning a business takes me away from my kids because we work long hours, but I'm really learning so much about being a businesswoman, and I appreciate all my clients. I have always believed that God doesn't give us more than we can handle, and a tough life sometimes makes us stronger. Our hair salon is now in its fourth year and doing better every year. My kids and I just welcomed my mom to come to live us. Seeing her getting older, slower, and forgetting more has really been hard on me, but I wouldn't change anything. I feel blessed that she chose my family to live with, and my kids are learning a lot from their grandma. I have more time with my mom than all my other brothers and sisters. I ask God every night to please let us keep her a lot longer, and I know God has plans for everything, including my life, my kids, and my shop. I am very thankful for everything.

~ Ngan N., 51-year-old

Sometimes it is the challenges and difficulties that propel us into taking great leaps forward. Like Ngan, we may not have a relaxed, reflective time as we race through the steps of the Equation for Transformation. Instead, if we do the hard work and have faith, we can be catapulted into our new lives before we even realize it. Later, we may look back and see that we are much happier now than we were before.

Here are some thoughts from Middlehood women as they muse about what is best about this time in their lives:

Being a lifelong learner, I am so excited about several new learning paths for me. . . . I hope I have time to explore all of these wonderful things I want to do!

~ Susan K., 51-year-old

I'm old enough to know right from wrong, but young enough to still have fun!

~ Shannon C., 40-year-old

Spiritually, I am growing in many directions at this time of my life . . . and have deep gratitude for the journey thus far . . . knowing that change occurs when we rise to it and push aside our fears to dare to reach for our dreams.

~ Terry L., 56-year-old

I am enjoying and dreading my daughter growing older. I'm able to live an authentic life of being my true self and living on my own terms. I'm not trying to keep up with anyone else.

~ Sharon T., 48-year-old

I'm brave, I'm up to life, I don't play by the rules (or more accurately, I'm not bounded by what I hear should be the rules). I'm competent, effective, powerful and playful.

~ Gaile B., 45-year-old

The sun will rise—that is the promise. We will emerge into the light to a new time of growth. The question is, are we ready?

So if life is like climbing a mountain, let us look at where we are: halfway up the mountain. We are no longer the youngest or the last in line; now we are in the middle. We know this because we can see the lights of those in front of us, we realize that we also carry a light, and we see that the road behind is crowded with those who follow us.

Reflection Questions

- What in my life is coming to an end? How can I honor that process and help it happen?
- Where in my life am I waiting? How do I deal with waiting? What methods can help me be patient and open?
- What new doors are opening? What new ideas are taking shape? What do I need to do to activate them?

CHAPTER 4

Whose Body Is This?

The thing that is really hard, and really amazing, is giving up on being perfect and beginning the work of becoming yourself.

~ Anna Quindlen, *Being Perfect*

I really don't think I need buns of steel. I'd be happy with buns of cinnamon.

~ Ellen DeGeneres

"WHOSE BODY *IS* THIS? WHERE DID *my* body go?" we wail in frustration at all the mysterious physical changes that happen in our forties and fifties. After decades of our own peculiar mix of strengths, weaknesses, and predictable patterns, we suddenly find ourselves inhabiting bodies we scarcely recognize. The whole process of suddenly not knowing what our bodies are doing is disconcerting, sometimes even frightening.

Suddenly, an old friend has become a stranger, causing confusion and fear. Changes are happening: hormones, accumulated wear and tear, injuries. It is called aging. Cells do not reproduce as fast, joints wear out, muscles lose elasticity, metabolism slows, and on and on. Did we really think this was not going to happen to us?

Truthfully, yes, a part of us has always doubted that we too were going to get old and decrepit. Is there a woman alive who could honestly say she has not harbored the hope that *she* would be the exception? The nature of being alive is to think that what we have been in the past is what we will be in the future. Oh, and we try, don't we? We dye our hair, exercise more, get face-lifts, take hormones, go on diets, and try in every possible way to stop the inevitable changes. Does it help? Sure it does, in some ways. Being active, taking care of ourselves, eating well, getting hormonal and other medical assistance if we need it—they all help us feel better and look better. Do these measures stop the aging process? No. We are not old yet, but at this stage, the aging of our bodies is much more apparent.

What do I miss most about my younger body? The way it looked before it needed ironing!

~ Sandy R., 58-year-old

Listen to what other women say:

But I've always had trouble with my left knee; why is my right one hurting now?

~ 53-year-old

I have never had trouble with my weight. I still eat well and walk every day, so where did this belly come from?

~ 50-year-old

I used to love to stay up late and enjoy the quiet after everyone else went to bed—now I'm lucky to make it to 9:00 p.m. without falling asleep on the couch!

~ 47-year-old

I used to struggle to get up early for work—now I'm wide awake at 4:00 a.m.

~ 51-year-old

Sometimes when I'm teaching, I just go blank and for the life of me, can't remember a word I was going to say or the name of a student I've known for months!

~ 62-year-old

I have a whole closet full of wool sweaters because I used to be cold all the time. Now, even in the middle of winter, the most I wear is a cotton sweatshirt!

~ 50-year-old

One night, just as I was about to go to sleep, I suddenly felt my heart beating kind of hard. I was afraid I was having a heart attack!

~ 56-year-old

The element of surprise in the changes that are happening to us can create a feeling of powerlessness, that somehow we cannot trust our bodies anymore. We remember some of those feelings from puberty, when we had pimples, gained weight, started wearing bras, and got our periods. For many of us, this was a dreadful time. We constantly compared ourselves with our friends, worrying that everyone else was beautiful and comfortable, and somehow we were not doing it right. We lost our energy, grace, and the unselfconsciousness of our childhood. Suddenly, we thought we were ugly. We cried a lot, got angry easily, never got enough sleep, and felt caged and frustrated by all of the expectations and responsibilities we had. Sounds kind of familiar, doesn't it?

When we were younger, we did not have the knowledge or experience to tell us that some of what we were feeling was caused by hormonal changes. Maybe our mothers would say, "You're growing so fast, you'll be clumsy for a while, but then you'll be okay. You'll grow into yourself, don't worry." We derived some comfort from the words, but we had no experience to reassure us. Now we have that experience behind us, and we are in another tumultuous time of change: perimenopause and menopause. And now it does help when older women say, "It won't always be like this. You won't always feel this way. It is a change, you'll get through it. But . . . you'll be a little different on the other side."

Oh, menopause—the period in my life when I did "pause" from my relationships with men. It was the best of times and the worst of times. I spent ten years on my own discovering who I was while my body persisted in blessing me with hot flashes, sleepless nights, and restless leg syndrome. My personal philosophy was that if I survived becoming a woman, I could certainly survive changing as one. I refused drugs and replaced them with hundreds of pages of personal reflection, massages, counseling, books on self-development and spirituality, and many wonderful friends. As with all stages in life, it passed—leaving behind a stronger, more knowing, and happier person.

~ Susan McC., 58-year-old

How can the Equation for Transformation help us accept our changing bodies? First, there are some things we *must let go.* We have to let go of using younger women as models for what is beautiful and strong. We have to let go of what we used to be able to do and what used to be true for us. We need to listen to our bodies about what they need *now*. If we are tired, we need to rest more and be more active. If our sleep patterns have changed, we need to accept sleep when it comes, even if that is a nap or going to bed at 7:00 p.m. If we have gained weight, we need to eat what our bodies are really hungry for and stop thinking of how it used to be. If our joints hurt, we may need to find physical activities that help us. It is tough—we know it is. We do not want to make all these changes. We want to stay the same as we have always been. But we cannot—it is as simple as that. We are not doing a better "job" of aging by denying what is happening. The only people we might impress are younger people who think they can avoid the changes that come with getting older. Everyone our age or older knows what is happening, and they are not fooled.

Until I was in my early forties, I was an avid athlete. Because of the excessive high-impact exercises I had done all my life, I wrecked both my knees and can no longer do any high-impact exercise. Now I do light weight training, Pilates, and walking. However, these types of exercises don't have the same effect on keeping me as fit and toned as I would like. Mind you, I'm also older now, and this old body probably doesn't respond the same as it did in my youth.

~ Donna S., 55-year-old

Slowly, full of complaints, we enter the middle place. Once we stop living in what used to be, we are ready to look at what is. This is where we take a deep breath and step into reality—our reality. During this waiting time, we can do an honest inventory of our strengths and attributes, and create a list of what we can do or have always wanted to try. We will likely be sad to let go of familiar activities, but if we have done the work of letting go and have created emotional space, we may find ideas we had never considered. We can apply these same techniques to assessing our physical appearance and find new ways to accent what is beautiful. Mainly, we try to remember that if we stay stuck in how it used to be, we'll miss out on how it could be.

When I was in my midforties, my twenty-year relationship ended, and I closed my business. With emotional work, the grief lessened over time, but I still held a deep hurt and anger. Ten years later, I found myself dealing with my dad and his declining health. I went to doctor's appointments with him and kept tabs on all his various health issues. During this time, I developed a spot on the outside of my left breast. A little voice kept telling me to get it checked out. I'd been concerned about my dad, but now I needed to listen to my own little voice. I got checked and the spot turned out to be nothing. While I was at the doctor's, I had a mammogram and found out I had breast cancer. As I was preparing for surgery and treatment, I read a book about the fourth chakra (heart) and breast cancer. It talked about old loss and anger in relationship to breast cancer. I consider myself a rational individual and even a bit of a cynic—but when I read that, I had a very visceral feeling, like a finger had hit a nerve. To me, having cancer was a wake-up call to really deal with my life and let go of things that I was still holding onto ten years later. Being diagnosed with cancer of any kind is always life changing, but it can be a self-affirming journey. I feel that my diagnosis saved my life, and because of the work I did after that, I am now a much healthier person.

~ Teresa S., 61-year-old

Like many of us, Teresa was taken by surprise by her health scare, but she used the experience to help her clean out years of accumulated grief and anger. Letting go of old ways of being and old images of ourselves is hard emotional work, but it is necessary so that, like Teresa, we can assess where we are and find new ways to be healthy. This is the work of the Equation for Transformation, and Teresa was fortunate that she had the opportunity to turn a frightening diagnosis into a new and richer life.

Hormones Talking

Let us talk about our hormones because they are definitely talking to us!

When we were young women, many of us tried to hide the discomfort we felt during parts of our menstrual cycles. Imagine what our lives would have been like if we had not felt it necessary to do that. It would have been lovely to stay home for a couple days each month, wrapped up in something soft and warm, drinking tea and napping. Instead, we took pills for cramps or water weight and put on our "I'm fine" faces so that no one would know we felt weepy or cranky or half sick. We carried on as though we felt fine and would never admit to any but a few trusted loved ones just how hard that was. If we showed our discomfort or stayed home, we risked not being taken seriously in our work or in the world. We would just be dismissed as being "on the rag." If we were honest with ourselves and families, we could admit that we were not making up feelings when we were menstruating. Rather, whatever we were feeling was intensified—a small frustration felt overwhelming or a small sadness, devastating. For a few days each month, our bodies and emotions were far more sensitive than at other times. Our hormones were definitely talking then.

Our hormones have been talking to us all our lives. They talked to us during puberty, and they talked to us during the decades of our fertility. They talked to us when we were pregnant, when we were lactating and weaning, and they are talking to us now. Most of us probably have no idea of how much our hormones control our bodies. When they start changing, nearly all systems are affected—physical, for sure, but also mental and emotional—more than we realize. It is important to listen when hormones talk because they convey vital messages that are part of a bigger change process.

One of the most important things we can do for ourselves at this time is to talk—say things out loud to our families, friends, and doctors. Many women are accustomed to suffering in silence, but when we do that, we miss out on helpful information we can learn from others.

One afternoon, a friend and I were talking about life and getting older. Since I'm normally a pretty upbeat and positive person, I was talking about how disturbing it was to wake up in the middle of the night with my brain just running in circles and worrying about everything. I wondered if something was wrong with me. It was the first time I had put words on those particular feelings and said them out loud. To my amazement, my friend understood exactly and had had a similar experience. She called hers "busy brain." As the conversation continued, I realized I'd never thought about it, but I could see how it was a pattern. It was my hormones talking.

~ Tally F., 54-year-old

Talking to other women can bring a sense of relief. Knowing that other women have similar experiences normalizes what we are feeling. What might have felt like a terrifying moment in the middle of the night becomes an annoying moment that can be calmed with a gentle, "Oh, that again. I will give it some thought tomorrow and see what I need to do." We each have our own specific concerns, and the worries in the middle of the night will not stop, but it does help to know we are not the only ones.

Perimenopause and Menopause

In her book *The Wisdom of Menopause,* Dr. Christiane Northrup writes that "around age 40, women's bodies begin perimenopause, the transition leading to menopause (the point in time when you stop menstruating permanently)." She states, "Many women sail through 'the change' without any symptoms at all, but others experience a wide range of symptoms, all of which have physical, emotional and psychological aspects."

Perimenopause is a long process of fluctuating hormones that profoundly affects every system in our bodies. Some of us start perimenopause in our thirties; others do not really notice anything until our forties. It starts slowly and progresses until we reach menopause, the end of menstruation. The rule of thumb is that we are officially in menopause when we have gone a full year with no period.

What are some of the symptoms of perimenopause and early menopause? These symptoms vary with each woman, but likely we will experience at least some of them.

- Changes in our menstrual cycles/cessation of periods
- Hot flashes
- Weight gain
- Emotional swings
- Aches and pains
- Heart palpitations
- Wrinkles
- Slower recovery from injury and illness
- Eyesight changes
- Memory blips
- Tiredness
- Sleep problems
- Rising cholesterol and blood pressure
- Less interest in sex or no interest at all

- Changes in hair, including texture, color, thickness, hair loss

Any or all of these changes begin during perimenopause. At first, we might not notice because the changes happen only occasionally or for short periods of time. When we are still cycling regularly, we might chalk up the odd symptom to stress or tiredness, and then forget the next month when things go back to normal. As perimenopause progresses, however, we notice more ups and downs: a normal month, a weird month, a few days of irritability and sleeplessness, then calm and peacefulness. Sometimes we are clear and ready for whatever life needs from us, then suddenly we are overwhelmed and confused. After a while, we do not know what to expect.

One night my husband rolled over to cuddle with me. When he put his arm around me, he jumped back and said, "Wow, you're hotter than the ass end of a rocket!" Well, thank you, honey, I love you too.

~ Anne C., 59-year-old

Weight isn't as much an issue as all the aches and pains that have crept up and become normal for me. It's like I'm just wearing out! I'm noticeably weaker and stiffer overall—the last time we went canoeing, we decided we needed to switch to a lighter kayak because it's too hard lifting the canoe on top of our car. There's an indignity about all this that I'm finding hard to take. Intellectually, of course, I understand what's happening: that I live a too-sedentary life and that my hormones are shifting in a way that also affects my joints. But emotionally, I've been in a bit of a temper tantrum about it—angry and fearful. I do not like the reality, and I do not like the solutions that are, admittedly, well within my grasp because of the time that exercise "steals" from other, more interesting pursuits.

~ Cindy L., 49-year-old

We should understand that perimenopause is a time of change and that, for our sense of well-being, we should listen to what our bodies and emotions tell us. Holistically, what happens in one area of our body or mind affects the rest. For instance, not sleeping well affects our energy level, weight, blood pressure, emotions, memory, and our body's ability to heal. Gaining weight changes our energy, sexuality, blood pressure, cholesterol, aches and pains, balance, strength, relationship to food, and sense of attractiveness. If we are out of balance in any area, everything else will likely be affected.

I'm not exactly happy with my body, but still it serves me well . . . more aches and pains, wrinkles and weight. It doesn't bother me too much.

~ Teresa S., 56-year-old

Once we are fully in menopause, the rapid pace of ups and downs slows. Now we find that the changes we have experienced do not go away after a few days or months. Many women are delighted when they stop having periods—no more worries about pregnancy and no cramps or backaches every month. We are happy when the hot flashes and mood swings slow down or disappear. We begin to take stock of what is gone, what has changed, and what is coming.

I found going through early menopause initially quite disappointing because it meant the end of the possibility of bearing children. However, I've learned to accept the fact that we will never have natural children and am now quite okay with that. In fact, I rather enjoy the freedom that being childless has allowed me and my husband. On the other hand, not having menstrual periods was very welcome. My periods had always been extremely heavy, so I wasn't bent out of shape over leaving that aspect of my womanhood behind. Now that I'm postmenopausal, I rarely even think about it and am comfortable with being postmenopausal.

~ Donna S., 55-year-old

No matter where we are in the perimenopause/menopause cycle, there is nothing simple about this time in our lives. Here in Middlehood, we are in the evolutionary/revolutionary process of change. We are all going to go through it, whether we want to or not, but we can establish some control over the process. We can make it conscious, give it a little direction, and grant meaning to the changes instead of just blindly stumbling through.

At the age of forty, I returned to college to complete my elementary education certification. It was a big deal—I had made the transition from a ten-year career with a nonprofit agency and was interested in teaching. I began in the fall, and I was so nervous—over-the-top nervous. I started to have hot flashes and felt like I was internally combusting. I went to my doctor and mentioned that I thought I was beginning menopause, but she told me that I was too young. I went home and called my mom—of course! She told me that she had gone through menopause young too. I went to a natural healer, and he got me started on herbs for hot flashes and menopausal symptoms. I made sure I took care of myself and I made it through!

~ Jeanne S., 41-year-old

Balance

One thing that is helpful in managing our changes at this time is applying the concept of balance. Anyone who has studied dance, a martial art, yoga, or any sport knows that we need to learn how to find and keep our sense of balance. Nothing is possible if we are in constant danger of toppling over. Where does that balance come from? It comes from our center—from our core.

Searching the internet with the phrase *strengthen your core* yields more than seventy thousand hits. Many health and wellness organizations and services agree that strengthening our body's core, which includes the muscles of our abdomen, back and pelvis, is crucial, because when we are strong and in balance, we have a powerful way to help protect ourselves from injury and pain.

After years of knee pain and decades of waiting for emerging technology and the courage to reach the point of going bionic, I now have two new knees, one four-month-old knee and one six-month-old knee. Each new step, both literal and metaphorical, brings me closer to pain-free and the chance to see more of the world, people, and places. Each new degree of motion means I have triumphed yet again. When, in most of our lives, do we ever get that kind of chance for ever-unfolding gratitude, surprise, and wonder at the incredible human machine that is us? Altogether, each success, each new thing I can do on these bionic knees, is a real blessing. I am alive and kicking high!

~ Cherie S., 62-year-old

Just as we strengthen our physical core, we must, especially in Middlehood, strengthen the core of who we are, the center of our lives. Finding that balance, clarifying our highest priorities and guiding principles—our core values—and acting on them is vital for health and well-being. Over the years, we might have ignored or sacrificed deeply held beliefs for other people or obligations that seemed worthwhile at the time. Perhaps we did that for money or status or work, perhaps for relationships, our children, or our families.

Certainly, compromising our core values, bottling up our self-esteem and spirit cost us—in energy and power. As young women, we had huge reservoirs of raw physical and emotional power to bounce back from injuries of any kind. We could live on coffee and willpower when necessary. We could put the demands of our spirits and hearts on hold while we developed other parts of ourselves. But . . . no more. Here in the middle of our lives, that behavior is harmful to our health, possibly even life threatening. No one is immune to the challenges and losses that occur in life. If we are strong in the core of our bodies and strong in the core of who we are, we will have resources to protect us and carry us through the hard times.

When I was young, strength meant a kind of physical endurance and the ability to push through anything. Now it is much more a quality of spirit.

~ 55-year-old

Trees demonstrate this principle of core strength every winter. As the temperature drops and the hours of daylight decrease, sap begins to pull out of the leaves and twigs, sinking deep into the trunk and roots of the tree. The harshness of winter might snap off twigs and branches, but the tree will survive because its core is safe and alive. Bushes do the same thing in dry climates. In a serious drought, all of the visible life in a bush can die back into part of a root, where it waits until the rains come, and the bush can grow again.

Each of us is like a tree with a central core that must be fed and nurtured. Our leaves and twigs are all of our external bits—a part of us for sure—but in the course of any life, we will change jobs, interests, and roles many times. Just as when storms injure or break the tree's large branches, we will survive to grow again if we have kept our crucial heartwood alive.

Doing so is not always easy. There are a million ways that we are not in harmony with ourselves. We make decisions and commitments, but then we forget. We profess beliefs but act contrary to them. Many of these contradictions occur when we try to embody beliefs that are not really ours. Ideas and behaviors that do not ring true with our essence create dissonance or disharmony that will surface with dramatic clarity in our Middlehood years.

Using the Equation for Transformation can help with the process of unifying ourselves. At the heart of each of us, a few true things remain at every age and phase of our lives. Middlehood is a natural time to either reconcile our contradictions or find a way to live peacefully with them. If we do not, the conflict will suck away our energy and sense of purpose.

We may need to let go of some external things in our lives. If we cannot do that in healthy ways, we could lose our balance and become ill or depressed. Not only external demands pull us away from our core; our own worries do the same. We do much better finding ways to accomplish this passage by listening to our intuition and taking action to nurture and build our cores in whatever way we can.

The fear of running out of time to be Me looms larger with each passing day. I'm not afraid of getting old, but there's still so much I want to do in life. . . . Hopefully, one of these days I'll figure out how to balance my life.

~ Anne C., 59-year-old

I am living with integrity—that is, from my center, with my activities aligned with my core passions and values. I am comfortable with who I am—my assets and my limitations. I am not concerned with how others view me as before or whether I am living right by others' standards.

~ Holly S., 51-year-old

The next time an infomercial pops up on TV and urges us to "strengthen our core," we should take the message to heart. Some of those exercises are for our bodies and some for our values and beliefs, but all of them are important. We must not forget our core—it literally holds us up and keeps us in balance.

Energy

Another way we can manage this transition is examining our energy: how it works, how it has changed, and how we can use it to do what we want.

Many people going through a major transition need to slow down or pull back from normal activity. Ironically, just when many of us feel that need to let our sap sink deeper into our cores, our lives get busier and more complicated. Everybody pulls at us: children, grandchildren, aging parents, spouses, partners, friends, not to mention careers and volunteer work.

In all natural cycles, there is both a time and a need to pull back from external demands, to rest and rejuvenate. This is true in daily, weekly, and monthly cycles and also in life cycles. As we pass through Middlehood, profound changes happen on every level. We need time to digest the changes, to understand and incorporate them into our re-forming selves. Our society is not tuned to those natural cycles, so often we live like flower bulbs in artificial light, forced to bloom at unnatural times. This takes a terrible toll on our energy. When our internal voice says, "Slow down, sit awhile, let's think about this," and we cannot, the next voice we hear says, "This is just too much!" That overwhelmed voice, the "too much" voice, speaks with increasing desperation the longer we ignore it.

When I began performing as a mime, I spent hours alone exercising, practicing, and creating stories. Before a performance, I went into silent mode for an hour. After my son was born, I exercised while the meatloaf was in the oven and imaged stories while vacuuming. When he was six months old, I accepted a mime gig. I had a great plan that didn't work. I fed him, then handed him off to my husband for my hour of silence. I had just finished my makeup when I heard him crying. My husband brought him back, and when he saw my painted face, he screamed. I talked and sang until he calmed down enough to nurse, and just as he fell asleep, the stage manager called two minutes. I stood behind the curtain, closed my eyes, and breathed. I stepped on stage and let everything else go. The performance went as well or better than ever, and after that, my preparation adjusted to circumstances. If I had an hour, I took it, but if it was thirty seconds, I made it work. Time was not important. Concentration and focus were, and that was something I could control. I don't do much mime anymore, but there is full-time work, community and creative projects, seven grandchildren, family and friends. That all requires attention. I close my eyes, and breathe.

~ Sharon N-D., 61-year-old

Many of us have noticed that the way we express our energy is changing. If we persist in clinging to our past ways of doing things, we can easily overspend our energy. Learning our new limits in practical ways is important to our physical and emotional health.

When Carrie and I were in our early forties, we owned a small landscaping company. Our crew was made up of women and men ranging in age from early twenties to midforties. Many times, the truck would arrive at a work location to unload bags of mulch, and the younger people would enthusiastically grab a bag or two and start walking across the lawn before they realized they had no idea where they were supposed to be working. They'd walk back, still carrying the bags and wait for instructions. Carrie and I would just shake our heads, noting that not a single person over forty would even touch a bag until we knew exactly where we were going, and then we would walk in a straight line directly to our work area. "I'm still as strong as I've always been," Carrie said, "but I don't waste my energy now. I work smarter!"

~ Maggie W., 43-year-old,
and Carrie M., 41-year-old

Maggie and Carrie's story offers a good lesson for Middlehood women: many of us are as strong and healthy now as we have ever been in our lives, but something is changing. Maybe we do not have the endless supply of energy we used to have, or maybe we have to pace ourselves differently. Those of us who used to sprint through our lives in short bursts may find that these days, we are more comfortable with longer, slower, more sustained efforts. Conversely, those of us who were marathoners may be happier with intense high-speed intervals and more naps! Many of us discover that we are far more focused than we used to be and prefer specific tasks, rather than trying to do several things and feeling scattered. And some of us own up to the fact that we *can* do everything we used to, but we *don't want to*! Climbing up on the roof to clean the gutters or painting the eaves is just not as much fun as it used to be.

Many of us do not want to discuss how our energy is changing as we move into and through Middlehood. There is a real fear that we might be dismissed as "getting old" or not taken seriously anymore. Each of us must face our changing energy in our own way. In order to do that, we must listen to ourselves, not hang on to how we used to be out of habit or fear.

For the most part, I am who I wanted to be. I also find that, right now, the energy I am willing to put into new things is minimal.

~ 51-year-old

Everything has to pass this test: Is "fill in the blank" how I want to spend my time? If the answer is no, I don't do it. The only things I do out of duty are for my immediate family. No one else gets that level of energy from me. My energy and time are for me.

~ Janis S., 52-year-old

Sexuality and Intimacy

Sexuality is as varied and diverse for Middlehood women as it is for women of any age. Sexual energy is not only physical but also mental, emotional, and spiritual. Here, as in so many other ways, when our bodies change, our feelings change, and we are called to explore new avenues of pleasure and intimacy.

I have lost weight in recent years, I feel attractive and active, my sexuality has become heightened, and my husband and I have an active, exciting sensual relationship. In many ways, I feel better and look better than I have in years!!

~ Nancy S., 52-year-old

Many of us may be enjoying a very active sex life and find that sexuality is still a fulfilling, exciting part of our intimate relationships. As time goes on, we may find that we express our sexuality differently. If it takes longer for us to become aroused, we have more time to explore and be creative with another or ourselves. For some women, sexual intimacy gets easier at this time of life, especially if there is no more worry about getting pregnant. For other women, sex is no longer our preferred way of being intimate, yet intimacy is still something we long for. Open communication with our intimate partners is essential to enjoying this time in our sexual lives.

> *My libido seems to have gone on vacation for the past few years, and I'm regretful of that. But my partner is accepting and understanding.*
>
> ~ Susan McK., 63-year-old

As we fully enter menopause, some women admit to a common theme; as one woman states, "I have more thoughts of sex than actual sex!" Depending on our individual makeups and the health of our intimate relationships, we can feel either a profound sadness or a great sense of relief when we realize that most evenings, the thought of sleep is more attractive than anything else.

> *I am not pleased with my body right now. I am not happy about gaining weight and being less active, yet I don't seem to be making a priority of the changes I need to make in this regard. I do see myself as a very sensual person. And I do see myself as a sexual being, but I don't always have the energy or desire to act on it.*
>
> ~ Elaine F., 54-year-old

For those of us who find ourselves alone in the middle of our lives, the questions of sexuality and intimacy can be just as complex. Without an intimate partner, our feelings can range from peaceful acceptance to desperate loneliness. Again, we must be clear about what we are missing and what we are longing for. Is it a need to be hugged or held? A longing for the soothing touch of warm hands? Is it a fear of being alone without help or support? Is it deep communication and sharing, or a sense that someone really knows us and the full story of who we are? Nothing can fully replace a committed partner or spouse, but it does not have to be an all-or-nothing situation. Maybe we can initiate deeper emotional connections or share more personal conversations with our family and friends. Our willingness to be flexible and open in ways true for us is critical to our well-being.

> *Mentally, I feel very good. I feel more passion for my work and family than ever. My memory is not as good as it used to be (especially my short-term memory). Emotionally, I think I am very stable and stronger than ever due to life experiences. I feel like I have a lot to offer emotionally to others. I feel more connected to my spirituality than ever; time has taught me to feed my spiritual being more. Physically, I know I could take care of myself a little better. I could exercise more. The ways I cope in life are to turn to my husband, my mother, and my women friends.*
>
> ~ Carol S., 50-year-old

Health and Healthcare

Negotiating these changes in the midst of busy, complex lives is stressful. We know that! Modern medical research continues to warn us that stress is at the top of the list of health hazards, right there with smoking, unhealthy eating, and lack of exercise. Chronic stress throws our bodies out of balance, diminishes our resources, and allows what were previously only potential health problems a chance to grab hold.

Of course we are stressed—how can we *not* be? Even good things can be stressful: a new relationship, a better job, a new house, holidays, and other events. The body does not know the difference between good and bad stress, so because change and life are stressful, and we are in the thick of it, we are stressed. The key is how we handle the stress in our lives. Do we have the coping skills to face it head-on?

Sometimes things just pile up on me, and before I know it, I'm not sleeping well, not exercising, and eating junk. Stress can be very sneaky. It is important for me to find ways to keep my good habits even when I'm stressed. I'm working on it as best I can.

~ 46-year-old

My way of coping is that I usually cry a lot, then pray. Sometimes I drink.

~ Veda T., 60-year-old

What helps? Medication? Meditation? Hormones? Exercise? A noninflammatory diet? Yoga? More money? More sleep? More friends? Retirement? Kicking the adult kids out? Breathing exercises? Fewer responsibilities? Divorce? The list of possibilities goes on and on. What works for one may not work for another. The bottom line is that *all* of us need to learn to manage stress, and spending time and energy figuring out how to is not selfish. It is not overly dramatic to say that our lives depend on it.

Stress and stress-related problems are prevalent for women our age. Adding stress to the physical and emotional changes of Middlehood poses a potential health risk, so we must find and utilize healthcare providers we trust and who treat us with respect and concern. Some of us already have a whole team of resource people: various kinds of doctors, teachers, therapists, guides, and body or energy workers. Whether for an annual exam or a tune-up, we are not afraid to call when we have questions and concerns.

Some of us are part of the sizable group of Middlehood women who do not have a regular healthcare provider. Why is that? We are not afraid to go to the doctor when we are pregnant, and most of us are really good about getting our kids to the doctor when something comes up. We are famous for nagging our spouses and partners to take care of themselves and go to the doctor, so what happens to us? Why do we stop thinking of healthcare as a means of protecting ourselves and instead grow afraid? Why do we wait until something goes wrong before we venture out?

Strange, isn't it, especially for those of us who take care of children, grandchildren, and parents? We cannot possibly take care of other people if we do not take care of ourselves. We *know* that, yet we dawdle and postpone all the way to actually making an appointment. We have many reasons for delaying our own care, including cost if we do not have health insurance or good insurance. Making appointments for times convenient with work schedules or family responsibilities is hard. Getting an appointment with an appropriate specialist may take so long that we feel like giving up. These reasons are straightforward, but there are other, subtler reasons some of us have disconnected from professional healthcare.

One of the most insidious reasons may be that we are afraid we will be judged. There is a pervasive sense that much of what happens to us when we hit our middle years is our own fault, a punishment for past indiscretions. After all, we are the ones who ate too much fast food or smoked for all those years or did not jog in our twenties and thirties. We are the ones who made all the mistakes, so our punishment is to be sick. The truth is that many of us did not take good care of ourselves when we were young. We were careless with our bodies, got caught in addictions, or thought ourselves immortal. We lost our belief that doctors and healthcare providers were healers and instead viewed them as judgmental parents who would scold us for our mistakes. We are so afraid we will get bad news that we do not want to go at all. If we do go for an annual exam, we want only good news, not warnings about potential problems. We want them to say, "Your blood work is great!" so we can walk out of the office relieved that we are absolved for another year. Our heads held high, we say, "Look at me! I was good this year!" But when the doctor expresses concern about our cholesterol or blood pressure, we feel like we did something wrong and hang our heads and do not want to go back.

> *I remember when I was young, and my parents felt they needed to discipline me by pointing their index finger at me and telling me right from wrong. It was a humbling and scary experience, and always made me feel very small and stupid. Unfortunately, the same thing happened to me at a physician's office—not once but twice! I was having knee replacements, and the PA asked about my blood pressure. It had been borderline for several years. He and his accusing finger made me feel like a lying kid even though no doctor had ever prescribed blood pressure medication for me. That ridiculous finger thing has appeared in several other situations in my later years. What is up with that? Why do people have the need to belittle us as though the finger puts us in our place?*
>
> ~ Joan W., 59-year-old

Many of us fear that much of our health is controlled by genetics, so nothing we do makes any difference. This feeling that no matter how "good" we are, we cannot fight genetic markers, creates a terrible feeling of hopelessness. For example, cardiovascular disease is the number-one killer of women, and if we have cancer and heart disease on both sides of the family, we may think that we are doomed no matter what we do. While having genetic predispositions lets us off the guilt hook, the feeling of hopelessness prevents us from taking positive, life-enhancing steps to care for ourselves. But it is not hopeless—we must work in partnership with our doctors. When we have good relationships with our healthcare providers, we do not have to give up and give in to our family genetic history. We can take action to build on our strengths and minimize our weaknesses.

> *I recently learned I'm allergic to gluten and have cut it out of my diet. In less than two months, my thirteen years of fibromyalgia symptoms are nearly gone, along with terrible, debilitating digestive troubles. I've lost fourteen pounds and feel twenty years younger! I feel so much better that I've begun practicing aikido again. Since I became ill, I've only been able to work part-time jobs. I finally have my life back and am ready to work, but I don't want to sit at a desk, so I've taken a job walking dogs. Now that my body doesn't hurt all the time, I'm in love with the feeling of being alive again. Life is great!!*
>
> ~ Judy A., 55-year-old

Blame, shame, and hopelessness are completely ineffective ways to help us take positive steps in our lives. We do not blame our kids when they get sick or hurt; we immediately take them to the doctor to get help and care. But too many of us do not trust our healthcare providers. So what can we do? We can begin by finding a doctor or healer we really like, someone who treats us with respect, compassion, and intelligence. We want them to answer our questions and, in every possible way, become a partner and supporter in helping us maintain a happy, healthy life.

However, many of us feel overwhelmed by our healthcare system. Besides expense and inconvenience, we struggle with insurance or finding doctors who will take new patients. We feel rushed through appointments, or we are randomly assigned to doctors we have never met. The whole point of preventive healthcare is to have a place where we can feel safe, ask questions, get information, and not be afraid. We might have to try out several different physicians or healers before we find the one who is right for us. Does that sound like a lot of work? Maybe, but think how picky we are about finding someone to cut our hair. Lots of people are perfectly good hairdressers, but we would *never* stay with a hairdresser we did not like. We must not stay with a healthcare provider we do not like out of a misguided sense of loyalty.

As we find our way through the years of Middlehood, we will make many decisions about how to take care of ourselves. Many of those decisions will have to do with perimenopausal/menopausal changes. Some women choose hormone replacement therapy, and some, natural therapies. Many women have few symptoms or problems and opt not to take any medication or herbs. Each of us needs to choose from these viable options what *our* bodies need and what makes *us* most comfortable. Just because a friend got relief from her hot flashes by drinking soy milk or taking black cohosh does not mean that will work for us. Working with us as a team, our doctors and other healthcare providers can help us make informed choices, but no one drug or remedy works the same for every person. We must be willing to find what helps us.

As we make the passage into our Middlehood and beyond, we need to take our health seriously because we will have more to be scared and confused about: breast cancer, osteoporosis, and heart disease, for example. We have to keep our immune systems up and inflammation down, and that requires more than just annual exams or taking vitamins and supplements. We must also eat well for our bodies, find healthy activities that we enjoy, get enough sleep, join in loving relationships, and ensure that we make time to laugh and play and find some joy in our days.

When we were younger, we tended to think that serious illnesses, disabling conditions, or loss of physical abilities only happen to "older" people. All of a sudden, in my late fifties, with lots of friends now in their fifties, sixties, or seventies, the folks with serious health issues are us! Some people respond to that by becoming fearful, and allow their world and experiences to shrink, not because they are no longer able to move about in society, but because they are in self-protection mode. Ironic, isn't it? They are so afraid of losing their ability to live as they want, that they stop living freely anyway. I admire the people who grab at every opportunity to broaden their horizons and who take all kinds of reasonable risks. These folks don't defer anything because they have learned that next year, or even tomorrow, may be too late. No more waiting until "someday"—if you're in Middlehood, "someday" is today!

~ Tally F., 56-year-old

Education and Advocacy

Here we come! Women between forty and sixty-five number in the tens of millions in the United States alone, and we are a huge percentage of the adult population in many countries. Simply by the force of our numbers, we will continue to change the awareness, knowledge, and research about the needs of Middlehood women. In this way, we are educating our healthcare providers and the medical establishment. Research is no longer based on test results of men only. Women have different health needs, symptoms, and responses to medications and treatments.

Too many of us wait to visit our doctors until we are scared. We need to talk to our healthcare providers along the way and ask questions. When we explain our concerns, fears, or symptoms at our annual exams, and our physicians say, "Oh, that's just perimenopause," we cannot let them stop there. We need to ask more questions: "What does that mean? Is this normal? What might I expect? What happens next? Do other women experience the same thing? What kinds of diet changes, treatments, or exercises might help? Do I need to be nervous? What should I watch for? What causes this?"

One evening in my early fifties, I suddenly started to have a strange sensation of my heart beating faster and harder for no particular reason. Frightened that I might be having a heart attack, I called the doctor and was told to get to the emergency room immediately. I called an ambulance and arrived at the hospital, where I underwent a number of tests. When the tests didn't show anything except a rapid pulse, the doctor asked me more questions. When I explained my age and the fact that I was in perimenopause, he said, "Oh, well, that's what it is," and sent me home.

~ Susan K., 51-year-old

Even though Susan was not having a heart attack, the physician should have given her more information about perimenopause and about heart health. Healthcare providers sometimes dismiss women's health concerns, only to later find that the condition is serious. Prior to that experience, Susan had not known that heart palpitations were a common symptom of perimenopause. Of course, we should always check out strange symptoms, but having more information can save us from frightening and expensive experiences.

We cannot depend only on our healthcare providers for information; we also need to educate ourselves so that we can ask about new interventions. If we are lucky and still have our mothers, we can find out how Middlehood was for them and put together a medical history of the women in our families. We can read books and visit credible websites to learn more about health issues for ourselves and our families.

My husband had two serious heart attacks by the age of fifty-three. For the remainder of his life, he and I were partners in his healthcare, but it was the last ten years that were really problematic. During the last year of his life, he was in and out of the hospital fifteen times. The paramedics knew him on a first-name basis! As his caretaker, I was always observant, vigilant, and proactive during my husband's in-hospital and home care. I became an "instant expert" regarding his medications and his disease; that way, my conversation with the doctor was always more productive and meaningful. I did realize that each time we got home from his hospital stay, I needed a little break once in a while from the caretaking. I asked my friends for help, and they were happy to do so. As a caretaker, it is so important to take care of yourself too!

~ Sally V., 65-year-old

More than anything, we need to be our own advocates. We need to know our family medical history, ask questions, speak up and have an opinion, and educate ourselves and our families. Nobody will do that for us. Many of us learn to advocate for ourselves because we started out advocating for someone else, perhaps our children or our elderly parents. Now we need to do it for ourselves and to teach others to do it as well.

Those of us who currently have, or have had, serious or catastrophic health problems know that we must be our own advocate throughout the diagnosis and treatment process. More than anyone else, we know that collaborating with our healthcare providers will assist us in having a more positive outlook. We also know how important the support of family, friends, and community is to our progression to health and well-being.

Cancer. You never know how you're going to react when you hear that word spoken directly to you. For many women it brings tears, a range of emotions, doubts, fear, panic. If you do feel any of these, it's okay. Go ahead and cry or scream. You will have your own way of coping. It's okay. You may want to call everyone you know or keep it to yourself. Either way, it's okay. . . If you hear the word cancer, whatever your response, whatever you do, however you feel . . . any emotion is okay. This is a woman's prerogative.

~ Martha Lanier, *Pink Lemonade: Mastectomy Tips and Insights from a Breast Cancer Survivor*

As Martha says, there is no right or wrong way to deal with our health issues, but we can help other women by supporting them and encouraging them to take action for their health.

We are not powerless or simply at the mercy of unknown forces; rather, we are in a time of dramatic change. Although we may feel a deep sense of loss or grief that our bodies are no longer those of the young women we once were, they are not strangers or enemies. Here is where we can turn our attention from assumptions based on the past to exploration, education, and understanding of what we need to do to take care of ourselves now.

The question we posed at the beginning of this chapter is easy to answer. "Whose body is this?" It is *our* body, of course. It is *our* hormones talking, it is *our* fears and hopes; it is *our* histories and futures intersecting. Approaching and going through menopause and Middlehood is not a punishment or a signal that we are somehow broken and that the best of our lives is now behind us. Instead, it is a conversation that involves every part of us, and the choices we make and the steps we take now have everything to do with how we will experience the rest of our lives.

Reflection Questions

- What do I struggle with the most as my body ages? What aspects of my life are most out of balance right now? How can I remedy or find peace with these concerns?
- How is my energy changing? What are new ways to sustain it?
- How have sex and/or intimacy changed for me?
- What health issues do I have right now? How am I taking care of them? What do I know about my family medical history that will help me stay healthy?

CHAPTER 5

Truth and Beauty:
The Courage to Be Authentic

Heaven preserve me from littleness and pleasantness and smoothness. Give me great glaring vices, and great glaring virtues, but preserve me from the neat little neutral ambiguities. Be wicked, be brave, be drunk, be reckless, be dissolute, be despotic, be an anarchist, be a suffragette, be anything you like, but for pity's sake, be it to the top of your bent. Live fully, live passionately, live disastrously. Let's live, you and I, as none have ever lived before.

~ Violet Trefusis, 1918

The more honest you can be (with yourself and with others) about who you are and what you need to be fulfilled, the more likely you are to create a life that's right for you.

~ Suzanne Willis Zoglio, *Create a Life
That Tickles Your Soul*

IT TAKES STRENGTH, LOVE, AND A sense of humor, honesty, courage, and acceptance to live and grow in Middlehood. We have spent decades learning about ourselves and how life works. We have accomplished many—although maybe not all—of our goals, enough that we know what we really want in our lives now. We

67

also know we have made mistakes, learned things the hard way, and tried and failed at both inconsequential undertakings and those that really mattered. We have scars from those failures, but we also have the beginnings of true wisdom. We have found our voice—to speak up for ourselves and others. We are less afraid of what others think of us and more committed to standing in our own truths and being who we really are. Perhaps the process of becoming authentic is simply bringing our insides and outsides into agreement and connecting deeply with our essence, even as it changes. It is about taking care of ourselves in a way that empowers us but does not disempower someone else.

To be an authentic Middlehood woman is to accept where we are—full of joy and sadness, regrets, forgiveness, hopes, and plans. We accept that we are halfway up the mountain, with a long history behind us and dreams for the future still in front of us. As we work through the Equation for Transformation, we can embrace who we have been and—both loving and honoring that history—let it go and move on. We know what we have lost and what has passed, but with great courage and determination, we can focus on what is new to keep building our lives. Doing so, we will find that unexpected gifts begin to flow.

I turned fifty last December. It was a wonderful and exciting event. I felt I was starting a new chapter in life, which has endless possibilities. I'm free of many of the emotional chains I placed on myself in earlier years. I don't care much what others think of my wardrobe, my hair, or my disposition. And I care more about what I think of those things. I'm a nicer and friendlier person now. I feel attractive and beautiful—just for me, and sometimes for my husband too. I am extremely lucky to have the husband I have. Who else would have told me that, even on the hardest or worst days, I'm the best thing around?

~ Caron W., 50-year-old

Beauty and Attractiveness

As women, we have struggled with accepting our appearance all our lives. Now that we are in Middlehood, the challenges are deepening.

It's like people, even my family, think I'm broken! That being heavy means I'm broken somehow! They think I don't care about myself anymore!

~ Lynnette M., 55-year-old

Broken—what a good word to describe how society sees women dealing with some of the physical effects of perimenopause/menopause. There is a sense, as we enter menopause, that our function as women is now broken; a system that worked well is old or dying, and we can do nothing except fade into the sunset. Even we might believe that story on some levels. If we no longer think of ourselves and our attractiveness—our weight, hair, and skin, for instance—the way we used to, what should we do? Give up? Turn into frumps? Of course not! Instead, we adjust our thinking and let go of the past; we find new ways to define what makes us look good.

I miss perky boobs and having no cellulite on my legs! I used to be slender and leggy when I was younger (before kids). I still feel quite energetic but can't move as rapidly or gracefully as when I was younger, and that can be irritating.

~ Nancy S., 52-year-old

If we have made it into Middlehood, we know one thing for sure: styles, fashion, and images of beauty change—a lot. We have lived long enough to *know* this absolutely. Think about hair—we have straightened, bleached, curled, ironed, hot combed, cut, dyed, streaked, and spiked our hair. We have worn bobs, Afros, pixie cuts, braids, mullets, dreads, flips, and spit curls. We have wrapped our hair in orange juice cans or bits of cloth, used Dippity-do, volumizers, mousse, and hair gel. And clothes—well, go-go boots came and went (thank goodness!) and so did tie-dye and bell-bottoms—oh wait, they came back, didn't they? Are they in or out now? How about shoulder pads, leggings, torn sweatshirts? Loud sweaters, short shorts, Bermuda shorts, pleated slacks, miniskirts? Are pearls in or out? Pillbox hats are out, but we love some of those beautiful hats full of color and flowers that show up in church. What about scarves and head wraps? Fashions change so fast that we might actually find ourselves staring into the closet or drawer, wondering if it is safe to wear something we had just put away last season! And these are only a few of the fashion and style changes we have seen in our lives. Imagine what our grandmothers must have seen!

Now the harder question: what about our bodies? Cultural images of what is beautiful also change. We have struggled with this conundrum our whole lives. Those of us in our fifties and sixties remember when Twiggy replaced Marilyn Monroe as the ideal of white female beauty in popular culture. No longer was voluptuousness the standard. No longer did teen girls chant, "We must, we must, we must develop our bust," while swinging our elbows forward and back. To be attractive and stylish, we had to get skinny—no hips and no boobs. Those of us who did not fit this new standard of beauty—most of us! —struggled with our weight, our hair, our big hips, and our skin color to make sure we looked "right."

At the same time, our society began to idolize what was new and young. We started to throw things away instead of fixing them. Even worse, as we got older, and passed the dreaded age of thirty, we began to realize that the throw-it-away mentality was beginning to apply to people. Gone was the age-old respect for elders, gone was the appreciation of people and things that had lasted. If youth and newness were the ideal, what would happen when we were no longer young?

Do what you can to preserve what you have. It's not trying to be a younger version, but being the best version at the present.

~ Sharon T., 48-year-old

So what makes a Middlehood woman look good? Is it clothes? When we were sixteen, we thought we had to wear short skirts, style or cut our hair a certain way, use a particular kind of makeup or buy a popular brand of shoes to be beautiful. Sixteen-year-olds think that it is all about the outside stuff, about fitting in and looking like everybody else. But what about us now? Do we really still define what looks good on us by the current fashion, by what everybody else is wearing? Not so much. Most of us like to wear stylish clothes, but we now have a better sense of what suits us, regardless of a passing style. Finding those clothes in stores might be harder these days, but we have a clear sense of our own style, and we do not need to measure ourselves by everybody else. We can say, "I think that looks good on *me*. Maybe not everybody is wearing it, but I like how it looks on me."

We have always expressed ourselves through our clothes. We can make a statement with a t-shirt or a style. Do we wear a Hawaiian mu'umu'u because it is comfortable or because it connects us to something cultural or ancestral? Are we wearing a head scarf because we are having a bad hair day or because we have lost our hair from chemo or are we wearing a Nigerian *gele* (gay-lay) to celebrate our people and history? Do we wear skirts because our religious or work dress codes require it, because the men in our lives like them, or because we look great and feel great in them? Unlike when we were young, we are not bound to a few limited, transitory options to fit in. Instead, we choose our clothes and our style based on what is important to us. If we wear clothes that honor a religion or tradition, we do so happily. If we love fancy shoes or hiking boots, and opt to spend some of our extra money buying new ones, we can enjoy that. If we prefer to live in our jeans and sweats, that is our decision as well. The blessing of being in our Middlehood years is that we make these choices more freely.

Clothes do not matter to me at all, except that I will no longer wear anything that feels scratchy, tight, or uncomfortable in any way. No more suits with narrow skirts with cold legs in hose on winter days, shoes with any kind of pointy anything. . . . I could easily go the rest of my life and never buy another piece of clothing, except for underwear.

~ Kathy B., 61-year-old

What about hair? Color it or not? If gray hair means old, what about those of us who like how gray hair looks or who go prematurely gray? What about short hair? Long hair? Do all Middlehood women have to cut their hair to look good? Goodness, it is complicated! It is not our hair that makes us beautiful. We are experienced enough to know that fashions and styles will continue to change over time, and that gives us freedom to choose how we will look.

I am a physician caring for patients in the emergency department, a place of frenetic energy and life-or-death moments framed by vomiting, sore throats, and sprained ankles. My shifts are no longer adrenaline-driven sessions charged with visions of being the medical savior for an unfortunate trauma victim. No, my caffeine-fueled hours are often filled with a desire to just peacefully help out the quiet, friendly grandma with pneumonia while my younger colleagues tend to blood and gore. At fifty-eight, my energy level has dropped significantly, and I sometimes feel old and tired. Last month on a whim, I bought a box of hair color and made the streaks and patches of gray adorning my head disappear. What a difference I saw in the mirror! That box of joy charged my self-image, erased wrinkles, put a smile on my face and a jaunt in my step. Others also noticed the difference. Now patients ask me, "How long have you been out of medical school? You don't look like you have been practicing long." I only purchased one box.

~ Sheri K., 58-year-old

For most of us, somewhere in Middlehood, wrinkles will appear and lines deepen, breasts will sag and bellies thicken. Are cosmetic procedures—a face-lift, tummy tuck or Botox—the answer? Maybe. Some of us think it is worth thousands of dollars to have these procedures. Most of us though, see favorite celebrities with too much collagen in their lips or faces pulled so tight they look like masks, and wonder what went wrong. Does getting rid of wrinkles make a Middlehood face look young? Is there something more to our faces and bodies than the surface signs of Middlehood, something that tells about the decades of life behind us?

The first time I realized there was a change in my face was when I noticed those little up and down lines by my ears! I had noticed them on other people, but never seen them on myself. Darn it!

~ 48-year-old

Life changes us inside and out. Trying to erase the external signs of age does nothing to change the experiences reflected in our bodies. Every success or failure, every risk, joy, fear, and love are written in and on us. No amount of surgery will remove the steady look of experience in the eyes of a Middlehood woman. A face that has practiced smiling for forty or fifty or sixty years will still fall into the familiar lines where the muscles pull and the skin shifts. We are in the middle of our lives, and it shows.

When people say to us, "Wow, you don't look forty (or fifty or sixty)," are they really paying us a compliment? Young women and youth represent the standards of beauty by which we are supposed to measure ourselves—apparently for the rest of our lives. What if we stopped comparing ourselves with younger women? What if we responded to the backhanded compliment of someone telling us we look younger than we are by saying, "Hey! *This* is what forty (or fifty or sixty) looks like!" What if we decided to look *fabulous*, not young? How would that change our attitudes and decisions about appearance?

Many of us have long believed that popular culture and media images do not represent all women, certainly not Middlehood women. Despite cultural standards of beauty, something in us recognizes when a Middlehood woman looks good. It is not just about a pretty face or stylish clothes but about how we redefine beauty and attractiveness for ourselves.

I have always looked at myself as being an attractive and beautiful woman. The invisibility of the black woman has nothing to do with age. Unless you are Oprah Winfrey or Michelle Obama, I don't think people see black women. Black women have been diminished to a point where we are relegated to stereotypical roles on TV, the big sassy momma, or the wisecracking best friend, who is there with great advice, but no life of her own. I want to be seen, not because of what I look like, but because of my presence. I want to be acknowledged, not by someone looking right through me or gazing right by me to the next person. For me, it's being present. I want to know that I am a contributing person and member of society and that I have value, not only to myself and my family, but everyone else out there. It's because I am a black woman and a Middlehood woman both. I'm not twenty something, and I think it is all wrapped up in the cultural thing that is ever present in everything.

~ Sharon T., 48-year-old

We have learned over the last twenty or thirty years that being attractive is dependent on many things, but mostly on how we feel, not our appearance. Do we look good when we are tired, stressed, or sick? No. Do we look good when we are happy and smile a lot? Yes! Being healthy makes a huge difference in our appearance. Confidence is a big factor. It shows in how we walk and carry ourselves. Do we hold our head up or always look down? What about self-respect, openness, peacefulness, and self-assurance? In the long run, those inner qualities affect our attractiveness more than any of the media images we see.

I know I look good for my age, but what is attractive at 62? I don't have an internalized standard of beauty for this life phase, and comparison to my younger self doesn't take me to an appreciation for what I am now. I am not heavy, but carry 5-10 pounds more than I used to have, and somehow it doesn't matter very much to me. The focus now is on how I feel, not on how I look. The focus has shifted from the eyes of others to my own subjective sense of how I feel.

~ Kathryn B., 62-year-old

If popular culture decides what is beautiful, then no matter how old or young we are, most of us will not fit the image. None of us can compete with celebrities at this point in our lives—could we ever? —even with a personal trainer, a personal chef, and airbrushing. But if we define beauty and attractiveness for ourselves, we can think differently about how we are aging and spending our money. We can decide that we are getting older and better, instead of struggling to look younger. Imagine the gift that we would give each other (and younger women) if we stopped saying, "Wow, you do not look . . ." and instead, wished each other a happy birthday by saying, "Wow, you look fabulous!"

Visible/Invisible

I recently went into a local coffee shop and was surprised when the young man behind the counter looked right at me, smiled, and said "Hi! How are you today?" What was most surprising was my surprise! Young people used to smile at me and say hi, but that hasn't happened in a long time. Mostly these days, young people are polite, not really friendly. When did that change?

~ 55-year-old

Something like that has probably happened to many of us. It is not usually an overtly insulting comment or encounter, rather, just the feeling of being invisible. The sensation feels strange for many of us who have recently passed out of our twenties and thirties. We might be relieved that young men no longer call out or whistle when we walk down the street or try to strike up a conversation when we are busy. All of us like to pass unnoticed at times, but no one likes to be dismissed, passed over, or ignored simply because of our age.

I hate feeling invisible. It really started in my fifties. I wonder if it's part of what makes some women act like bitches as they get older.

~ Kathy B., 61-year-old

Human beings seem to like to categorize people, sorting them by age, gender, race, clothes, jobs, money, and other labels. We rarely realize what we are doing and usually mean no harm. What is harmful is judging others by those categories. One of the most common categories we make assumptions about is age. Those of us in Middlehood have already lived through a phase in our lives when we were judged because of our age: our teens. It drove us crazy! "They don't even know me; why would they think that about me? I am not like that!" No doubt, each of us made a comment like that at some time in our young lives because those judgments were infuriating and insulting. As we finally grew into our twenties and thirties, most of that age stereotyping stopped, and we forgot how it felt. Now, it is happening again, and we remember that feeling of frustration. "I am still me! Why can't young people see that?"

> *At fifty, I still kind of felt "with it." But at sixty, I'm like the oldest fart at school . . . and those young girls at school— the young teachers—it is like I'm invisible.*
>
> ~ Peggy H., 60-year-old

We did not understand when we were younger, nor did we realize that we made assumptions about older people. Now one of the blessings and challenges of this time is that we get caught in our own crap. We see that we are doing it too. How many of us have seen a group of teens at the mall or on a corner, laughing and acting silly, and thought, "Teenagers! When are they going to grow up?" Or we have heard ourselves think, "Hurry up, old lady, you're too slow." Ouch. We are just as bad as everyone else, and the very behavior that we resent is exactly what we are doing to younger and older people.

We make each other invisible when we generalize by age or any other label. But the gift of awareness in Middlehood can change us and, in turn, we can make a difference to others. Now that we remember how it feels, we can catch ourselves when we make comments about people based on their age. This helps us look at a person, not a stereotype. Suddenly, the teens who volunteer their free time on a project of ours become the funny, kind, smart people they really are. What about the older people we encounter? If we throw out our assumptions, we can actually see the impish smiles, hear the hilarious sense of humor, and listen to the stories of insight and experience with relish. Assumptions are empty—people are not.

When we stop making other people invisible, we are less invisible. When we speak to people we encounter, make eye contact or smile, the seeing is mutual—we see them and they see us. It does not have to be a big thing. We can simply say hello to the skateboarding kid who passes our house each day on the way to school. How about a smile to the Middlehood woman pushing her elderly father in a wheelchair? Perhaps we just momentarily acknowledge someone else, but we could also begin a conversation, even a friendship. We could give and receive a gift of more value than we can imagine.

————

Becoming Visible by Nancy Geha

I was at Denver International Airport, waiting to pick up a friend, and went into a shop to pass the time. As I looked at a beautiful picture on the wall, I noticed a Middlehood woman sitting on a couch in the back of the store. She was holding a cell phone, and her hands were shaking. Never shy, I smiled and said, "Now that's the life, sitting on a comfortable couch."

Visibly shaken, the woman motioned for me to come and sit beside her. As I sat down, I realized that she was about to burst into tears.

"Are you okay?" I asked.

She leaned over and whispered, "My doctor just called and told me I have breast cancer." Then the tears came, a flood of them.

As a former oncology nurse, I had seen this shock before. I took her hand and asked if she was there alone. "No," she said, "my husband is around somewhere." Calmly, I asked her if she liked and trusted her doctor. Will she get a second opinion? We talked for quite a while. Finally, her husband came around the corner and stopped abruptly, confused to see his wife crying and a stranger holding her hand.

He immediately rushed over to be with her as I got up and walked away. "God bless you," I said as I left.

———

We never know where people are in their lives. We cannot know the challenges or tragedies they face or the burdens they carry. But it does not take much to make another person visible. Those small steps might be a real blessing to someone else and become a remedy for our own feelings of invisibility.

Memory

We count on our memory for everything, and when it starts to change, we feel upset and frustrated. Short-term memory changes are among the first things we notice in perimenopause. Most of us are surprised and anxious that we can no longer rely on our ability to easily remember day-to-day things. We may still be comfortable with our long-term memories but worry that we are becoming like our grandmother, who was always saying, "I remember when I was a girl. . . ." We are going to have to adjust to a new relationship with our memory, because it is definitely changing.

I was driving by the cart corral at the grocery store, only to notice some poor lady left her pretty pink purse in the cart. Loved the color. Kept going a bit and thought to myself, "Oh wait, did I leave mine?" circled back, and sure enough—I am the poor lady!

~ Susan B., 47-year-old

It is so frustrating to be in the middle of a conversation and suddenly have no word for something we ought to know perfectly well. Not all of us have this problem, but plenty of us do. On a good day, we can laugh about it. On a bad day, we just want to thump ourselves on the head. Where have all those words and names gone? They are still in there, but they seem to have gone into long-term storage. Thank goodness for our Middlehood women friends who understand what is going on. They are perfectly willing to play charades with us as we wave our hands, acting out what we are trying to say. If we really get stuck, they might even start suggesting words to help us over the hump and back to a conversational pace.

My friend Jody was telling a group of us about her busy life. "I hate it when I'm so busy that I'm already late at 6:30 in the morning! This morning I was slowed up when I couldn't get my favorite pair of slacks . . ." The pause lengthened as we waited for the story to continue. "Oh, you know, um, . . . I'd washed them last night and I couldn't get them . . . oh, for heaven's sake, I couldn't get them . . ." Patiently we waited. Finally, in frustration, Jody blurted out, "Good grief, what I'm trying to say is that I couldn't get them . . . de-watered!" Laughing, I patted her arm and said, "Is dry the word you're looking for?" "Yes!" Jody cracked up, and we all laughed with understanding.

~ Jane T., 40-year-old

Some days I hate the fact that I can't remember common words now and then. Makes it difficult to get a point across to a client if I can't find the words. And it makes me feel daft. I'm not ready to feel or be daft. Probably never will!

~ Caron W., 50-year-old

Most of us would probably agree that our short-term memories are not what they used to be, but something else may be happening. How about those old memories that rise to the surface more and more often? Are we thinking fondly of old songs from the radio—the ones we can still sing word for word? Have we started to remember the smell of our grandmother's house; the kindness of a Middlehood woman when we were awkward teenagers; the excitement of running down the stairs on Christmas morning after Papa says, "Santa's been here!"; and watching *Gunsmoke* with Momma and sister on Saturday nights with yummy treats?

Where do these memories come from? What causes this resurgence? Are we unhappy and less interested in our present, dreaming of days gone by? Not necessarily. After decades of looking to the future, planning, organizing, and working for all the things we wanted to have and do, many of us are now bringing our pasts into our present. This kind of gathering process reaches back to times and places and people that we have loved, that have contributed something to our lives and who we are now. It is not just remembering, but re-membering—adding back lost parts to the whole. It is not that we have nothing to look forward to, no plans or hopes for the future, but maybe some of those decisions for our future have their roots in a bit of our past.

For instance, many Middlehood women find themselves with a growing interest in family history. When we were young, we were likely only interested in family history to find out if there were any pirates or presidents or heroes in our ancestry. These days, we might be interested in the stories of other characters in our family's past: the shop owners, slaves, soldiers, immigrants, farmers, survivors, and teachers. How did they live? How did they die? What kind of people were they? How did their choices affect those of us who came after?

Sadly, lots of us missed opportunities to learn about the experiences and adventures of our parents and grandparents when we were younger. If we waited too long, and our elder family members are gone now, we may feel a deep sadness that we did not ask questions and listen to the stories. Did we find out who all the people are in the old pictures? Did we write down the favorite recipes from our childhoods? Did we learn a bit of Italian, Lebanese, or Russian from our immigrant ancestors? Is it too late?

Certain people in my family were good at keeping family history and stories, and because they did it, other people didn't. My mother and aunt were recently trying to remember an incident that happened in their childhood. Why did it happen? What led up to it? How did it get resolved? They remembered that it happened but couldn't fill in any of the blanks.

~ Jan S., 55-year-old

None of us were born in a vacuum. If we are alive today, then our ancestors were survivors. No matter what they suffered, no matter how they died, they passed on their genes and their stories, and we are here today because of them. Perhaps, as we begin having memory blips, we can look to the past, as well as the present and future, for ideas about how to proceed. Maybe we need to re-story ourselves: to find out more about the family story that we are part of; to tell our own stories to understand ourselves better; or even to tell our own stories differently so that we can heal old wounds and move on with our lives.

By the time we reach Middlehood, we have had decades of experiences, loves, mistakes, and joy. Remembering is a mixed bag. Sometimes it increases our feelings of sadness and loss. But if we allow the sadness, we can experience the benefits of reconnecting with our old selves. When we can put our arms around our whole lives, we will feel a sense of its awesomeness. One human life, our life, encompasses so much in history, wisdom, power, and love. We feel gratitude as well as regrets. So although having trouble remembering words and names is irritating, perhaps an important process is under way. Maybe the resurgence of old memories serves as a reminder of what we have valued, what is still important, or old mistakes we do not want to make again. Maybe those old memories are rising to help us grow.

Power

As we redefine beauty and visibility, as we change our relationships to memories and the past, we also begin to redefine power and strength. We make trade-offs as we age, and the first place we might see those are in our physical activities. We let go of those activities that are no longer safe or healthy for us or can actively hurt us, and we take on new types. But power and strength are more than just physical. Over the years, we have learned about the power of presence, knowledge, and experience. We have learned about political and economic power. We are no longer beginners, young and inexperienced; we are becoming respected authorities in our professional fields and our personal lives.

What does power in our middle years look like? If no longer physical, where does it come from? The primary source is from our evolution into wholeness. When we let go of "shoulds" and "oughts," and settle into a sense of clarity about ourselves, we free up great stores of energy and power. We no longer waste time and strength fighting internal contradictions. We know who we are, so we do not have to struggle with the pressures of the world around us to conform to certain images. When we have confidence in our knowledge and experience, we are less uncomfortable or frightened to risk being a beginner again, to learn something new. With children and careers well launched, we can spend more attention and time with other work we want to do and other ways we want to develop ourselves. If we accept our diminishing power in the physical realm, how will we handle the increasing power coming from other dimensions?

> *Feeling powerful means being connected. Or maybe better put: being connected brings power into my life. This has been true throughout all ages for me. Right now I've chosen to step into the virtual along with real-life connectivity, which can be a challenge to learn, keep up with, and maintain balance. When things are good, I embrace the techno slice and living/working closely with people who live/work anywhere. It's a new life of social media and Google Analytics. I enjoy Skyping with kids I love and friends/colleagues for projects and creativity building. It's true that I prefer the real face-to-face to the screen face-to-face but find that my power is in being current and open to the new and different.*
>
> ~ Martha T., 51-year-old

To be authentically powerful, we must use the knowledge and skills we have acquired throughout our lives. If we are Middlehood women closer to the forty end of the age range, then we had much more support as girls to be anything we wanted to be, and we had a much greater expectation of being taken seriously no matter what we chose to do. Middlehood women in their fifties and sixties know the feeling of being pioneers, of toughing it out as the only girl in a boy's world. We know that even today, women are not groomed to assume power as men are. Instead, we grow into our understanding of authority and power in different ways. So it is important to celebrate the women who have already taken their skills and leadership out into the wide world, who are CEOs, senators, teachers, artists, professional athletes, soldiers, pilots, healers, entrepreneurs, astronauts, Supreme Court justices, and more. But it is also important to respect, support, and cheer on the women who spent their young years raising families and are now exploring new paths: new careers, school, projects, art, community service, and activism. Whatever process we follow, we must not be afraid to assume new roles of authority and leadership in our jobs, communities, and families.

Along with changing our expression of external power, we are changing our relationship to our internal sense of power. The primary change we make is developing a sense of realness and authenticity about who we are. When someone describes us as "real," they mostly mean that we are authentic and approachable. We have a "what you see is what you get" style about us. We are not faking anything. We are in the process of owning our whole lives, not just picking out the good bits and ignoring the rest. In our willingness to be honest, we have accepted ourselves, with no apologies for the life we have chosen. Neither do we apologize for having and stating our opinions. We find incredible freedom in that honesty and acceptance.

When we think about the most authentic people we know, a few strong characteristics stand out:

- They have learned compassion and forgiveness for themselves and others, and are not judgmental.
- They do not tolerate foolishness or waste time on things that do not matter.
- They are honest about who they really are, including strengths and weaknesses, and they communicate honestly, expecting others to be honest as well. They do not let

others deceive or lie to them. Their compliments are real appreciation, not flattery.

- They understand that life is often hard and many sad things happen, but they choose to focus on the positive. They know that, to a great extent, happiness is a choice and takes real work.
- They are okay with showing their emotions and understand that emotions are fluid. They are not afraid of anger, sadness, or love. They do not apologize for feeling a range of healthy emotions without getting stuck in a particular one.
- They have a terrific sense of humor about themselves and life in general.
- They will be the first to say that they are not perfect, but they are not paralyzed or humiliated by their mistakes— they grow from them. They give others the freedom to grow from their own mistakes.

Don't we wish we were one of those wise, authentic women? They sound terrific! Are we there yet? Maybe! For sure, all of us are working on it.

Gratitude

One of the most precious things we notice in Middlehood is our deepening sense of gratitude. Most of us took people and things for granted when we were younger, but we are less likely to do that now. We understand that seemingly small kindnesses have a profound effect on ourselves and others. We have seen how one choice leads to another, resulting in enormous changes. We have lost people we love and learned hard lessons about feeling regret for things undone or unsaid. All of these experiences, and more, have taught us to be grateful for the large and small things that have affected us and made us who we are.

Today, I am grateful for every breath I take, every experience, all the people who touch my life, the colors coming together in a quilt, family, memories, seeing Pikes Peak while driving to work, the hawk that greets me every morning, and having challenging work at sixty-three. I am also grateful for the lessons I learned growing up in Montana: when you get thrown off your horse, you dust your butt off and get back on. Life is like dusting your butt off. When you fall off, it is an opportunity to review, reflect, and decide. Getting back on is the way you face the challenges. Now, if it's a bad horse, you may decide to dust your butt off and try a new horse. I'm not stupid.

~ Patty B., 63-year-old

"I am who I always wanted to be"

Let us be honest. How many of us can actually say that we have become the women we wanted to grow up to be? Amazingly, a lot of us can say it and mean it. This is not a period in our lives where everything is going downhill. Many of us are happier and healthier than we have ever been. How have we done it? By facing up to the changes and challenges of Middlehood with courage, honesty, flexibility, and a profound commitment to living our own truth.

What is best about this time in my life is that I am grounded, finding the work I do fulfilling and balanced, a great partner, wonderful relationships with grown children and grandchildren, fulfilling friendships, stability, a great home. I have fulfilled most of my dreams.

~ Karla M., 51-year-old

We must never doubt how much courage it takes to continue to live this way. We have been chipping away at our fears our whole lives, and now more than ever, we have to stand up and speak out. Sometimes that means saying, "I am who I am, so just *deal* with it!" Other times, we just need to quietly go about our lives making the choices that feel right to us. It is not easy, but the gift of that work is being able to say, "I am who I've always wanted to be!" Are we happy all the time? No. But we do feel a sense of wholeness, rightness, and balance in our lives. When we look back down the mountain trail we have climbed, we can see how we have grown, who and what we have loved, learned, and brought into the world. From this perspective, we realize that we may not have done all that we dreamed we would do when we were young (one life is definitely not enough), but we are living true to our vision of who we really are.

Not all of us have this clarity right now, and none of us have it all the time. Sometimes we get thrown off course and feel lost. We thought we knew who we were and what we were doing, and then suddenly, we did not know anymore. It could be that our last child just left the nest, or we lost our job or savings or health. Whatever has happened, we know we are in the middle of something big, this transition from youth to elder, and we often feel confused. "Take a step and breathe" becomes a mantra for getting through the confusion.

Strength can take many forms. It can mean physical strength, and I certainly have my share of that. It also can mean that you're the voice of reason, the rock people turn to for support, advice, a helping hand, or a listening ear. It also means having the courage to take a stand, even an unpopular one, when you know that's the right thing to do. And it means having the inner fortitude to shut up and listen when someone just needs to talk and doesn't need advice, the sense of when to keep quiet.

~ Sandy R., 58-year-old

Whether we are happy or not, this is not a time to put our lives on automatic pilot and cruise into the sunset. We might have to let go of our familiar, habitual ways of doing things and, once again, try something new. We can feel overwhelmed, but this is a choice place in life, not a resting place. We need time to think and absorb all that is going on, but sooner or later, we will need to take action, and that action will likely require us to make some adjustments.

We have the power to change, to refocus and recreate ourselves as necessary, but we have to use it. Even the willingness to change makes us more flexible and that makes us less fragile. Nowadays, flexibility in our thinking and self-image is as important as flexible muscles and joints, because it is the best protection against injury and damage. Middlehood is a time of extraordinary possibilities, and we have the power to say, "I am who I have always wanted to be." If we honestly cannot say that right now, we must ask, "What do I need to do?"

Tucked away inside each of us is a sense of ourselves that is timeless and ageless. Most of us do not see ourselves as any particular age unless we are comparing ourselves with someone younger or older. We just are who we are, with the experiences that we have had and the lives that we have lived. But—and this is important—most of us are keenly aware that we no longer care for pretense. We are far more likely to say what we think or express our honest feelings. There is clarity and coherence between what we believe and how we act, and we do not need to hide our feelings anymore. In that way, we are more visible, more powerful, healthier, and in a profound way, more beautiful. What does it take to live an authentic life? Ultimately, being authentic is not about fame or fortune; it is not about accomplishments or ownership. It is about the truth—our truth—and whether we let that truth guide our choices.

Reflection Questions

- How are my definitions of beauty and attractiveness changing?
- In what ways am I being more authentic—taking care of myself in a way that empowers me but does not disempower someone else?
- In what ways am I better than I have ever been? In what ways am I not?

CHAPTER 6

Women and Mountains II

*I've been absolutely terrified every moment of my life—and
I've never let it keep me from doing a single thing I wanted
to do.*

~ Georgia O'Keeffe

*Our deepest wishes are whispers of our authentic selves.
We must learn to respect them. We must learn to listen.*

~ Sarah Ban Breathnach, *Simple Abundance:
A Daybook of Comfort and Joy*

WHETHER WE SCALE A STEEP SLOPE or wander a winding trail, we
are well acquainted with the challenges and joys of climbing our
personal mountains. Over the years, we have witnessed glorious
vistas and stunning sunrises as well as dark clouds and sudden
storms. At times, we have lingered in alpine meadows full of
flowers; at others, we have struggled to overcome a rock fall that
has blocked our path.

Looking back, we are often surprised, even amused, to discover
the qualities that elbowed their way to the front in our efforts
to get through a particularly difficult patch. We have needed
strength, courage, and confidence, but when we most needed to

break through an old limitation and find ourselves in a new land, the critical factor that rescued us was our stubbornness, wild imagination, talkativeness, or bad attitude.

So often we judge ourselves by what others have said about us. Were we told that we were a crybaby? That we talked too much? Were we told to stop acting like a boy? That we certainly had a high opinion of ourselves? All of the negative judgments we have heard through our lives have contributed to the fears we carry within us. Here in Middlehood, we can choose to step beyond those old walls by willingly challenging ourselves.

———

Cindy and the Wolves by Jane Treat

Cindy Lollar was part of a group of women I was taking on a wilderness retreat. A day and night of the retreat were planned as a solo: a time alone in a mountain forest. The whole group was nervous about the night part of the solo, especially Cindy. She had never spent much time in the wilderness under any conditions—certainly not a night alone in the mountains! She knew little about the animals of the area and looked a bit faint when she found out there were bears in the region.

We met once every week or two for a couple of months before the retreat. I taught the group fire-making skills and gave them information about staying safe from animals, cold, injuries, and getting lost. Despite the information, Cindy seemed very afraid. She talked a lot about her fears: of the animals and the cold and being alone. She worried that she might get hurt or lost. After a while, the other women stopped saying much about their fears because Cindy's seemed so much greater. All of us, including Cindy, worried that she would not be able to make it through the cold November night alone.

We set up camp in a national forest in the mountains of western Virginia, and everyone began their twenty-four-hour solo at dawn the next morning. The day was gray and gloomy, threatening snow. Two days before, it had been in the fifties; now we were lucky if it was much above freezing. I hoped the quiet time of the day was being good for everyone, but of course it was the night time that I worried about. It was going to be really cold when the sun went down! Was Cindy going to make it?

The next morning I was up early, excited for the participants to return and anxious to hear their stories—especially Cindy's.

Cindy wasn't the first person to tell her story. She sat quietly while two others told about their time. It was no surprise that the cold night had been a big challenge for everyone. When Cindy began to tell about her time, she seemed nervous. Her voice grew high-pitched, and she talked very fast.

First thing in the morning, she collected firewood and to her amazement, actually got her fire going! Pretty proud of herself, she stayed warm and comfortable all day. She wrote in her journal for hours, thinking about her life and all that she wanted to do. Then it started to get dark. The mountains loomed over her, and dry leaves rattled in the wind. The woods rustled and crackled with the movements of small animals. Alone in the dark, Cindy huddled by her fire, staying close to the small pocket of light and warmth as the mountain cold grew and the last of the light sank away behind the hills. The dark hours trickled by. She played with the fire, adding sticks and watching the sparks, and all the while listened intently to the sounds of the night around her.

Suddenly, she heard large animals crashing through the woods on the mountainside across the creek. Cindy scrambled to her feet and stared towards the side of the mountain. Blinded by the campfire, she couldn't see anything but the small circle of light around her . . . and then the howling started! With a shock, she realized what she was hearing—wolves! And they were howling and running fast down the hill, straight for her! She grabbed hold of a tree and desperately tried to remember her safety instructions.

Should she run? No, no, no—that was the worst thing.

Was she supposed to climb a tree?

Think, think, think, what was the right thing to do for wolves?

Should she lie down and play dead? Stand very still?

The wolves jumped the creek and got closer and closer.

What to do? What to do? Hide in a log?

How many were there? Do wolves eat people?

As they closed in on her campsite, she stared wildly around for somewhere to hide or some way to protect herself. Almost panting with fear, Cindy did the only thing she could think of. She reached into the fire, pulled out a burning stick . . . and went out to meet them,

"And then for some reason, the wolves turned the other way and ran off," Cindy finished, and shyly looked at us.

We stared at her in stunned silence. Not one of us took a breath or uttered a sound while we contemplated the power of her story.

Of course, there were no wolves in the Virginia mountains; what she heard was a pack of hunting dogs. About 10:00 the night of her solo, I heard dogs baying off in the distance. It was an eerie, almost haunted sound echoing off the hills surrounding us. I hiked up the dirt road to a spot above the area where some of the retreat participants were camped and found a guy with a pickup truck and searchlight. He told me that his coonhounds had run off, and he was trying to get them to come back. The dogs continued baying from across the creek and up the side of the mountain. They were moving fast through the trees, and I realized they were running right near Cindy's camp. Of course! After a few minutes, the guy drove slowly on up the mountain, finally rounded up his dogs, and left.

I waited on the dark road above Cindy for a long time, fully expecting to hear her signal whistle calling for help. When it didn't come and didn't come, I headed back to base camp and left Cindy to finish her night alone.

Cindy did not know about any of this, and it did not matter. What she knew for sure was that she was alone in the dark and the cold, and she heard wolves coming for her. She did not become paralyzed or collapse when her life was on the line; instead, she made her stand with nothing more than a burning stick and every ounce of courage she had.

We had all made a terrible mistake. We had believed that Cindy was weak because she talked about her fears and that the others in the group were strong because they had not. Cindy taught us something important about the true nature of courage. Fear is not the same thing as weakness. Ultimately, it is not whether we are afraid or even whether we express our fear that matters. All that matters is what we do with it.

It is often hard for us to tell the difference between being afraid and actually being in danger. We may carry our mountain of fear inside, as Cindy did, and never realize the reservoirs of strength that we have. Only when we step out of our familiar safety and face our darkest fears with nothing more than a bit of light do we realize that we also carry a mountain of courage inside. To our great surprise, what we may also discover is that facing wolves, actually going out to meet them, is the safest and most liberating thing to do.

Reflection Questions

- What have I done in my life that took courage? Where did I get my courage?
- What has been a wolf at different times in my life?
- What have I used as a burning torch?
- What is my response to the idea that fear is not the same thing as weakness?

CHAPTER 7

The Ones We Love: Spouses, Partners, Children, Dating, Widowed, Divorced, Empty Nest

I believe that commitment is essential in a relationship, but not only the commitment to stay together. Each partner must commit to respecting, understanding, and supporting the other on their particular path through life. And, of course, love allows partners to make this journey and to travel together with passion.

~ Ana Nogales

Before I met my husband, I'd never fallen in love. I'd stepped in it a few times.

~ Rita Rudner

FOR MOST WOMEN, MIDDLEHOOD IS A time to redefine all of our relationships. We are working hard to figure out where we are on a personal level, and part of that work includes sorting out who we are with all of the people we love. This natural winnowing process happens because we vividly understand that all relationships take time and energy, and we seem to be running a bit short of both. We do not have time for fluff in our lives anymore. When we were younger, we could hang out with anybody whether we knew them well or not. No more! We barely have time to spend with our dearest ones, so why in the world would we squander any of that precious time with people we barely know? Once again, we find ourselves in between our pasts and our futures, puzzling over who we used to be and who we are now. Some of us are questioning every relationship we have.

This questioning requires a level of honesty and attention that can be both freeing and upsetting. Some of us are able to easily let go of the past, stand in the present, and flow into the future. Others hold on like terriers to a past that is slipping away without our permission. Most of us are a mix—sad for what is disappearing, calmly realistic for where we are presently, and hopeful or fearful about where we will be down the line.

No matter where we find ourselves today, it will likely be different tomorrow or next week or next year. The one sure thing is that everything is in flux, and this time of life is no exception. Those of us who grew up in large families or always had lots of friends may find ourselves in a much smaller circle of close companions now. If we were often alone in the past, we may yearn for close relationships and discover that we are now ready to do the work to make that happen.

As we have grown from children through adolescence and into our adulthood, we have found that our circle of loved ones has grown and changed. Who are all of these people that we love? We may find ourselves with a multitude of relationships, new and old, near and far. If we are in primary partnerships or marriages, if we have children still at home or who we see often, if we are meeting and falling in love with our grandchildren, we know that our relationships take an enormous amount of time and attention. These relationships are undergoing immense changes as we and they pass through life stages and emerge in new, uncharted lands. How about our parents and siblings? How have our relationships with them changed? And our friends? Where are they in our current circle? There are no easy answers or even universal descriptions for where we find ourselves now. Whatever the changes are, we are in the rich, fertile time of Middlehood and have the benefit of insights and resources from the past. They can add to our creativity and energy to enhance the circle of loved ones who support and inspire us.

Intimate Relationships

Married? Single? Widowed? Divorced? Isn't that what all the forms ask? It is hilarious to think of our intimate relationships reduced to those few designations. Do those four words even begin to encompass the complexity of our closest relationships? Is our relationship even covered by those four words?

That complexity is further compounded by the profound changes of Middlehood. We may feel less intensity, passion, or frenzy in our intimate relationships, but they may also be less fragile because of that. In many ways, we are stronger, calmer, deeper, and richer, and hopefully that makes us more trustworthy and more accepting than we used to be. We are different from when we were younger; inevitably, we will grieve what is gone, but let us not forget to celebrate what is better.

As we ride the occasional roller-coaster of new emotions and needs, it becomes vital that our intimate partners and spouses support and encourage us. This is no easy feat, but it is necessary to sustain our relationships through this time of change and into the next phase of our lives. So does a husband really understand what a Middlehood woman is experiencing? Of course not—not in an empathetic way, at least. He might be supportive and kind, but he also might just throw up his hands, saying, "Let me know when you feel better." But then, can another woman always understand what we feel and need? Of course not. No matter how loving she is, she could need support herself and not have the emotional space to reach out. We each struggle to balance and rebalance many facets of our lives during Middlehood. There are no simple solutions for any couple, but we all need love, laughter, compassion, and patience from our significant others.

If our relationship is working well, we can assist each other through our inevitable life changes. This is only possible with honest communication. We might simply say, "I'm really having a hard time today. I'm hot, I'm cold, I'm feeling kind of crazy, I need some time by myself." Expressing our needs this way bumps up both people to a greater level of loving detachment.

When we were young, we thought our partner's feelings revolved around us. If they were happy, we had made them happy; if they were upset, we had done something wrong. It takes maturity to realize that we do not cause other people's happiness or upset. Of course, we can contribute to the blessings or challenges in someone's life, but mostly, we are responsible for our own feelings. If we did not learn that when we were young, it will become clear during perimenopause.

A Middlehood woman's body and emotions have their own particular needs. Unless we are actually experiencing a health problem, the best anyone can offer is love and support—but there is no fixing what is going on. We might ask, "Can my partner/husband let me be wherever I am—with my hot flashes, sad memories, determination to try something new, or whatever? Can s/he just love me and do what is best for me in the moment, like send me off for a hike or draw a hot bath?" Perhaps one of the hallmarks of a maturing relationship is that we give up trying to fix things and learn how to let go in loving, supportive ways. Strange as it seems, perhaps the secret to a successful relationship in Middlehood is a combination of this loving release and a deeper, renewed commitment.

What is happening that pushes us to make these decisions, especially about our relationships? Middlehood women are beginning to understand that our most important, long-lasting relationship is with ourselves. At this critical time in our personal histories, we cannot let things slide. We know we do not have forever, and we are trying to figure out what is most important to us. We are willing to do the work necessary to keep our relationships growing, but most of us would much rather be alone than in a relationship that is harmful or limiting. For many of us, these feelings might be new.

When we were young, we fell in love with some aspects of the other person, qualities we shared or qualities we lacked, and they became the center of the attraction. As time went by, we began to fill out for each other, blossoming into far more complicated beings than we had first realized. During this part of the couple journey, we began learning more about the support and challenges we could provide each other.

So how can our present relationships metamorphose into sustainable, loving partnerships that will continue to grow with us into our elder years? We must speak up about what we are really feeling and thinking. If we are struggling with feelings about our aging faces and bodies, the underlying worry might be that we will not be valued or loved if we are not attractive. Whether we are vain or not, our culture promotes this fear, so we have to deal with it. If we are losing some of the vital sexual energy we used to feel, we might be anxious that we are failing as a lover or that we are not "in love" with our partner or husband anymore. Speaking the truth about how we feel can help uncover our deeper concerns and needs. Putting them on the table makes it possible for us, as a couple, to work on real solutions.

We will both struggle with aging and its complications in our own ways, but can we be there for each other? In order to defuse our fears and worries, we must be able to talk honestly with our husbands and partners. Only then can we get the support and reassurance we need to let go of how we used to be and accept where we are. Of course, our partners and husbands need to be able to reciprocate. Can we design a future together that allows each of us to grow into the changes we need without losing track of or impeding each other? To do that, we must find a way to embrace the changes even if they are uncomfortable. If we do not, we will find that our relationship becomes more and more unsatisfying and frustrating.

For instance, we can use the changes both of us are experiencing as opportunities to deepen or expand our language of intimacy. We can start with basic communication skills:

- Remember who each of us really is, not who we wish we were.
- Know what is meaningful to the other, even if it is not meaningful to us.
- "Hear" our partner's nonverbal ways of expressing love, particularly if s/he is not much of a talker.
- Remind ourselves that vulnerability, patience, and trust are the foundation of loving, enduring relationships and marriages.

It is vitally important that we keep our private language and code words—the simple words and reminders of past experiences, shared laughter, deep knowing—that we have constructed over the years. It is equally important that we stretch our creative sides and find new unique, loving ways to express imaginative and romantic connections. If we are both willing to open our hearts and do the work, we will embark on a powerful new chapter in our couple story.

My husband and I spent years arguing over money. It was an old disagreement that periodically came up and caused a lot of frustration for both of us. The real breakthrough came when we learned to stop the discussion before it became an argument born out of our two different perspectives. The solution was simple: we needed to acknowledge that the differences were just who each of us was, and those differences didn't need to be resolved. Nobody needed to be fixed because neither of us was broken.

~ Susan K., 45-year-old

Could a younger couple have discovered this truth? Maybe, but more likely the wisdom that allowed Susan and her husband to stop arguing came from years of love, struggle, and communication. If we are able to sail the stormy seas of changing needs and feelings, and come through to a place of love and commitment over and over, we may find that we have never been so happy. When we both try, we can work through the challenges of our differences with love and practice.

We know from decades of life experience that we cannot make someone else change who they are, any more than they can force us to change. We can communicate, negotiate, and compromise, but no amount of cajoling or arguing or manipulating is going to turn us into someone we are not. Hopefully, by this age, we know ourselves well enough to know our boundaries—what is negotiable and what is not. And, if our relationship is long and healthy, it has stretched over the years and has plenty of room for both of us.

Not all of us will be in a long-term relationship that can survive the tumult of our changing circumstances and feelings. Sometimes our husbands or partners will not have the flexibility or courage to grow into new and deeper relationships, and sometimes we will not. If we are too tired or fearful, or if we have not done the healing from old wounds that allows our vulnerability to grow, the challenges may be too much for us. If we are unclear about what we want or unable to express our longings, we may find our relationship on the verge of collapse from confusion and unspoken needs. We must then ask the question, is the relationship worth enough to face our fears and learn the skills we need to move to a new level of intimacy? We can find ways to learn new skills, or we can let the relationship go, but we cannot stay suspended between the possibilities. The energy of this time will likely push us to choose.

We know we have lots of love to give, but we also know we are not going to do the pretzel thing—no more twisting ourselves into various shapes, hoping that one of them will be perfect enough to guarantee the other person's love. Nope, not anymore. Now we stand for ourselves—a little shy, a lot hopeful, but determined that we can be ourselves *and* have a relationship.

Dating and New Relationships

How about those of us starting new relationships here in Middlehood? Is there anything in the world that pairs hope and excitement with anxiety and fear like a new relationship? Many Middlehood women who are presently alone may have thought that they would continue to be alone for the rest of their lives. Surprise! Maybe not. Women who begin new relationships at midlife are an optimistic sort. We have spent years learning about ourselves, overcoming limitations and fears, accomplishing goals, and building a life that matters. To willingly invite another into that space and take a chance on love again is a huge step.

I raised my sons as a single mom from the time they were four and six. We were a good team, a close family. I dated some during those years, but I joked (or not) that I wasn't single, I was triple!

~ Pam F., 58-year-old

I had been alone for a long time. I'd gone through all sorts of different stages about being single: relief, depression, loneliness, and finally an acceptance that my life was good the way it was. I had good friends, good work, and in most ways, I was happy. And then I met someone—on the Internet! I couldn't believe it was happening to me—on the Internet, no less! It was so complicated. We lived far apart, and neither of us wanted to move. Slowly, we deepened our relationship, worked out the complications, and I moved to be with her. It was one of the hardest and best decisions I ever made!

~ 45-year-old

It is going to be a challenge—especially for Middlehood women. Can we be stubborn and set in our ways? Of course we can. Do we have our own style and way of life—and does the other person? Absolutely! Do we know what we want and need? Are we clear about our edges? Well—mostly. At least we try to be. It is unlikely that a little known part of us is going to rise up like a sea monster from the depths and surprise us with some desperate need we did not know we had. But we still must tackle the process of bringing two huge lives together and melding them into a workable unit.

Sometimes I just feel lazy that I would have to put so much effort into forming a relationship. You can't just jump into a relationship and everything is great. You have to have a beginning. And sometimes I feel like I don't want to. I don't want to bring men in and out of my life, and the adult mature thing to do would be if I were in a relationship, I would introduce my daughter into it. But still stuff happens. I don't want her to have an example of a revolving door. I'm not setting out to put my life on hold until she's older, but when she is older in high school, I will feel freer to give myself permission to go do things. I would be open to someone stepping in unexpectedly right now.

~ Sharon T., 48-year-old

We might find ourselves facing different puzzles than ever before. For instance, combining the furniture might be more complicated. "But I want that chair to be in the living room—it was my mom's!" If Mom is gone now, her chair might matter a lot more than our previous furniture style of early American concrete and boards. Where will we go on vacation? If one or both of us have elderly or ailing parents, we might take a trip to see the folks more often than a romantic cruise. Sex and intimacy? Yes—still a precious part of our lives, although we probably cannot stay wrapped in each other's arms as long as we used to, what with that sore shoulder, aching back, or hot flash!

One of the things I discussed with my date last night was the difficulty we have as we get older, that we have more habits, likes, and dislikes that might not "fit" with another person . . . we have had some buttons pushed in the past. New people may not see the land mines until they've crossed the boundary. I had two dates cancel last weekend, for different reasons, which is fine. . . . I didn't have a back-up plan, but other alternatives were readily available for my attention. There was a time when I would have been so upset, it would have ruined my week. Not anymore. Maybe that's the joy of midlife. We mellow. The fact is, I have a life, and I'm glad that I do. I don't drop my girlfriends like a hot potato when I have a boyfriend. I've had more than one friend do that to me, and I just don't think that's the way to lead my life. . . . It's a matter of priority and balance. Once a man proves to me that he is a keeper, I just plan better so that I get to spend time with everyone who has meaning to me. Codependence is not a goal! Been there, done that!

~ Sondra S., 55-year-old

Inevitably, whether we are in a long-term relationship or a fresh new one, the circumstances of our changing selves will play a piece in how we design our couplehood, both now and into the future. Those of us who have been in a couple for a long time know, without a doubt, that two of the most valuable relationship tools are kindness and a sense of humor. Both are vital for a successful Middlehood relationship.

What If It Is Not Working?

What if our marriage or relationship is not working? Even if we are very unhappy, many of us will face hard choices at this point. For any couple, the combination of internal and external forces can make it difficult to sort out priorities. Any number of situations could develop. For instance, one of us might lose our job, or our children may be in a particularly stressful time. The idea of raising the children alone or trying to survive on a single salary is almost unthinkable. We may feel caught between two bad choices, unable to see any other options. Sometimes we know we need to leave if we are in danger of being harmed in an abusive relationship or have been betrayed by our spouse or partner. Imagining ourselves alone in the world is terrifying, emotionally and financially, but the support of family, friends, and helpful groups and organizations can assist us to make the steps to freedom and safety.

I am the type of person who, once I am in a committed relationship with someone I love, am as loyal as anyone can be. I try to do whatever I can to work things out in rough times. After seven years with my partner, I started to feel like something was going on. We fought a lot, and I thought maybe we were growing apart or just going through a rough patch as all couples do. I didn't realize her bizarre behavior toward me was because she was having an affair.

*When I knew positively about it, I kicked her out, and our
relationship was over. It took time to get over that loss, but
she will never know that her cheating and leaving was the
best thing that ever happened to me in the long run. I have
a wonderful partner now who loves me and is like night
and day from the previous one.*

~ 50-year-old

What about those of us in relationships with no danger or
betrayal, but also no joy in being together? What if we cannot be
honest and open with each other? What if our interests and dreams
have changed, and we have little in common anymore? What if we
feel like we are drowning or cannot put a finger on what is wrong,
and spend a lot of time worrying about the relationship with no
idea how to fix it. That dynamic may be the most difficult, but we
must work to recognize where we are and, if we can, find ways to
communicate with our partner or spouse.

Questions and Doubts

All Middlehood women have bouts of questioning and doubt
about nearly everything in our lives. We are in the midst of massive
changes, and the uncertainty is powerful. Sometimes we will be
paralyzed by this uncertainty, and at others, exhilarated. If we
have doubts about our intimate relationships, we can guarantee
that we will find fear and guilt and hope all mixed together. There
are many factors to consider and one of the most confusing is
our worry about being selfish. Many women worry about this to
varying degrees, and as a result, might be more likely to give in
rather than stand up for our own opinions or needs.

We have to ask ourselves honest questions. Am I telling the
truth about what I want and need? Am I staying only because
I am afraid to go? Am I feeling like a failure as a woman, wife,
partner, and lover? Have I got expectations that no one could live

up to? Am I really listening to what my partner/spouse needs? If we are not getting along right now, what are we fighting about? Sex? Money? Future plans? Emotional needs? Can I recommit to this relationship, or am I done?

Even in the best of relationships, not everything flows easily. We are so busy rearranging and shuffling our priorities that we both can get confused and stressed. If we are in a loving dialogue with our spouse or partner, we can support and encourage each other, even though we might not be going through the same issue at the same time. If we can detach from the other person's struggle and anguish, being loving and supportive is much easier. When one partner or spouse is determined to shift to a new place, and the other does not want change, the relationship may feel like a weight holding us down. Many women worry about being selfish in this case, but we must keep track of the deep process of life change that is happening.

This time of change is not just about our menstrual cycles. We are changing on every level: physical, emotional, and spiritual. Our whole life and worldview are changing. If we are *not* questioning who we are, what our lives are about, what our work means, or whether we are in a sustaining relationship, then we are not paying attention. Our fears are enormous, but so are our needs to grow and thrive. We each decide how much work to do to try and deepen the connection with our partner or spouse so we can stay and grow together. All answers are legitimate answers if they come from the truth of our own lives, needs, and circumstances. Stay together, seek counseling, divorce, renew, whatever we choose is up to us. If the decisions are a true reflection of who we are and the questions we honestly have, then it is a positive process.

Many Middlehood women do get divorced or separated, and many others weather the chaos and find themselves happy in a relationship that works well. As a group, we are all over the map, from miserably stuck in a bad relationship to happily committed in a terrific one. Many of us are in the dating scene, and others are content to be alone. The important work is finding our balance in the midst of change. We have conflicting needs and desires sometimes—no big surprise—so we make the best choices we can based on what really matters to us. We have acquired many tools over the years that can help us now. For instance, we have learned a lot about how to stay true to ourselves with love and compassion for the other people in our lives. And we may be more able to walk away from situations that do not work for us—a relationship, friendship, or job—and walk toward what we know is right.

When asking ourselves questions about our intimate relationships, we can remember the principles of the Equation for Transformation. Whether we are ready to commit or recommit ourselves to someone, or we are pretty sure we need to leave, we must act with a sense of clarity and understanding about our choice. Mindlessly staying because we are afraid to investigate how we feel or bolting because we cannot think of what else to do will not move us forward on our paths. Either choice will add to the baggage and confusion we feel about our futures. Alone or in a couple, we need to do the work of endings, let go of how things used to be, clear up as much as we can of the pieces from the past that hold us back, and then be patient with the in-between place, before we can step freely into a new beginning.

Getting Dumped, Divorce, and Death

It is all very well to talk of our choices to stay or go when we are the ones considering it, but what if we get catapulted into the Equation for Transformation without our permission because our spouse or partner leaves us or dies? That is a whole different story. If that happens, we will be knocked off our path and find ourselves lost in the dark, wondering what in the world happened. When we are the ones choosing to separate, we have to grapple with feelings of selfishness, sadness, guilt, and failure, but we also have an underlying sense that we are taking positive, although difficult, steps.

Getting dumped, however, especially for a Middlehood woman, can be devastating, financially and emotionally. Our self-esteem goes right down the tubes, and we start doubting ourselves. "How could I be so stupid? What could I have done to make him/her stay? Was it because I'm too old or not pretty enough? Maybe if I'd said yes to sex more often?" Most of us find ourselves shattered, feeling helpless, hopeless, depressed, lost, and overwhelmed. We might embarrass ourselves by begging or making desperate promises. We might burst into tears at any moment or feel unable to function with any semblance of normalcy. A little farther down the road, we are likely to start feeling the fury of being betrayed by someone we loved and trusted. We might even ask ourselves the question, "Did they really even love me at all?"

This is a cataclysm, no doubt about it. And it can happen to a woman at any age, but it has a particular kick when it happens in Middlehood. After all, didn't we think we were too old for all that drama? Didn't we think we were settled? Wasn't our future planned out? How could we have been so blind to what was happening? Were we just kidding ourselves? In a nutshell, we thought we were past the ups and downs of young relationships and comfortably settled in for the rest of our lives. It is stunning to find out that we were wrong, and now we have to pick up the pieces and start all over.

My kids were just leaving the nest when my husband left me, and we got divorced. My familiar family roles were changing, so work was essential! At least there, I had one old identity I could hang onto. Both during and after the divorce, yoga helped a lot and so did friends, both old and new. What has really made a difference though is getting to the point where I could totally, completely, and unconditionally forgive my ex. Of course that means acknowledging my role in his dissatisfaction with our marriage. But now after several years, I'm going forward with my life. Lately, I've been writing about my best memories (and some of the not so great times too!) from the marriage. It's mainly therapeutic.

~ Carol H., 61-year-old

Women whose husbands or partners die have similar feelings. A great wailing of fear and loss pours out of us. What will we do? Alone? At this age? We rage against God and illness and our beloved and the injustice of it all. We alternate between numbness and feeling like our skin is on inside out. On the bad days, we are sure that we will never recover, that we will die of the pain.

Either case, death or breakup, is an emergency, and our first responses must be toward survival. We must control the bleeding, do CPR to make sure we are breathing and our hearts are beating. Our family and friends will recognize this emergency and help us survive the slowly ticking minutes of the first days and weeks and months. We might have to face difficult choices that we feel completely unprepared to make. Where will we live? How will we live? Do we have enough money? Inch by inch, we grope our way through the list of things that have to be done, and we will use every one of our resources: people who love us, therapy, prayer, work, exercise, creative outlets, strength, and resiliency.

Recovery from a devastating loss is work of heroic proportions. We have lost our center, lost control, and lost hope. We will likely have to return to the very core of who we are to find the path again. When such a loss happens while we are already in the profound changes of Middlehood, we will be coming from much farther down the road to get to the point where we can feel good about our lives again, feel like we have some control and are growing and changing by choice. It can be done and will be done if we are committed to getting our lives back.

When we experience death and loss, we each walk our own path—at least that was what I thought until my husband, Dick, died. The loss of companionship, shared dreams, and our daily ritual of walking were hard to lose. But the biggest loss was of knowing each other's story so deeply and fully. At the funeral, I found myself lovingly surrounded by an invisible community I had not seen before. Other widows welcomed me with care, love, and compassion. Although I walk this loss on my own, I am accompanied by those who have already been on this path, as well as many dear friends and family who are with me. The biggest change for me is allowing myself to receive this love and care from so many. Shattered with shards of darkness in this deep grief, I have also experienced great light from the love, compassion, and sense of community I am allowing myself to take in. My heart has broken wide open, and there, I have found a new sense of wholeness—that darkness and the light are both part of this wholeness. I am learning to walk with the great compassion and love I am receiving— from myself and from loving friends and family around me. Even strangers extend care and compassion!

~ Susan K., 57-year-old

The principles of the Equation for Transformation continue to work as we reassemble our lives. First, we deal with the most basic level of survival. Once we are safely rooted on the planet again, we can begin the work of growing. We start with what is ending— not only a relationship, but also the end of dreams, images of ourselves, and familiar ways of doing things. We have to grapple with powerful feelings of anger and grief. We have to find what is still true about us in the rubble. This is where the heroic work happens. It is a difficult process to put away what is no longer true, to let go of old ways of thinking about ourselves, but *pole, pole,* one step, one breath, we keep going. We have to dig deep with honesty and patience to find out what is really ours, the bedrock pieces of who we are, whether or not we are in a relationship. The work will take some time. How long will differ for each of us. Our need to function in the world with our family, friends, and work further complicates the matter, but we must take the time necessary to sort through the attics and basements of ourselves so that we can walk into the daylight carrying a box of truth.

At some point, we will complete the work of finishing what has passed; the terrible heaviness that weighed us down will be a thing of the past. Now we enter the stage of waiting in the middle place. The work here is being open, recognizing that we have choices, and being willing to wait until those choices are clear. Are we living where we want to be living? Are we doing work that matters to us? Do we want another relationship, or are we content on our own? These questions and more will float through on a daily basis. In the middle place, we have to hold these questions and carry them with us without jumping at the first thing that comes up. When we are ready, we will know, and the decisions we make, from freedom and strength, will be trustworthy.

As we rejoin our sisters and friends on the road through Middlehood, we may be surprised. Because we have faced and survived some of our greatest fears, we will likely have a much deeper sense of what we want to do with the rest of our lives. Would we have chosen such a path? Probably not. But if we are wise gardeners, we will turn the garbage and refuse of our pain into compost that will grow something brand-new.

I feel like I missed the joys of my middle years because life got in the way. I was widowed at forty-two and had six teenagers to finish raising: three birth children and three adopted. After five years, life was back on track, and I felt strong and capable. But over the next few years, kid crisis after kid crisis kept derailing me. Always I came up with a new plan, until my oldest child, my daughter who was most like me, was diagnosed with cancer. I had only one goal: to be totally supportive of her. A year into treatment, the cancer grew more vicious, and six months later she died. My life crashed. I thought, "Why bother trying to cope? A new crisis is only minutes away." And I was right—a few months after her death, I needed brain surgery. This was not the life I wanted to be living! My healing was a long, slow process, and I envied the women around me who were relishing new freedoms. When I'm asked, "When was your last period?" I make up an answer. I can't even figure out what year. Menopause was insignificant compared with everything else happening in my life. My biggest fear was that I would become a bitter old woman caught in the pain of the past. Through lots of therapy and support from good friends, I learned to laugh and enjoy life again. But it took years. When I felt back on track, I made a deal with God: I was owed some years back to compensate for the pain and for missing so much of the middle part of my life. Since then, I am getting those years back, and life is good. In many ways, I feel younger now than I did when I was in my fifties.

~ Kate L., 65-year-old

It may not have been a death or divorce, but few women have lived into Middlehood without having had to reassemble ourselves from some loss, disappointment, or failure. Were we laid off from a job that we loved? Did an old friend die and leave us alone with the memories from our shared childhood? Has our aging body or a chronic illness forced us to give up our favorite activity? Did we lose money unexpectedly and find ourselves with no financial stability? We have felt lost, broken, even shattered more than once, and each time we have had to recreate a life of beauty and meaning from the pieces of truth that remain. Perhaps the masterpiece of our lives is not a sculpture or painting, but a stunning mosaic made from all of those broken pieces! *Kintsugi* is the Japanese art of repairing broken ceramics with a resin that has powdered gold added. The cup or bowl is then more valuable than it was before it was broken. So too are our lives—the golden seams that now run through us are a testament to the depth and power of our ability to survive and recreate ourselves over and over.

Having Choices

When we find ourselves on our own in Middlehood, what do we call ourselves? Alone? Single? Divorced? Widowed? Each word carries with it a particular meaning, with roots deep in our culture and in our personal histories. Does *alone* sound negative, too much like *lonely*? Does it imply a failure of some sort, that we could not attract anybody? How about *single*? Do we embrace *single* to express our openness to the possibility of a relationship? If we are Middlehood women who have never had a long-term partner or spouse, do we even use a label? Some of us really dislike the term *divorced* because it is a constant referral to a past from which we are struggling to free ourselves. On the other hand, some of us embrace the term *widowed* for the same reason: we want the connection to a fulfilling, positive part of our lives. What about those of us in sexual relationships for fun without a need or plan to deepen that relationship into a partnership or marriage? What in the world is the term for that: *friends with benefits*? Once again, we find ourselves in a predicament of language. Finding exact phrases for the intricacies of our relationships is often difficult.

The important element here is choice. By exercising choice, we experience power and control over our lives. If we are desperately trying to find a mate, then we probably feel something missing in our lives, rather than feeling in control. If we are recovering from a terrible loss, we certainly do not feel powerful. Our generation is far more likely to repartner or marry again than our mothers' generation, but we are also far more likely to have divorced or separated.

If we are contentedly on our own with a life we have made that suits us well, then we are not suffering from loss or desperation. Some of us would rather not be in a relationship and have rooted deeply with our extended families and friends. Others have found our way to that place after a failed relationship or the loss of a beloved husband or partner. No matter the circumstances, the key is to stay true to our feelings and the path we are on, so we will find the way that is right for us.

> *I've never been married. When I was younger, it was hard to fit in with all my married friends. People kept trying to fix me up. But now in my fifties, I feel very comfortable and happy in my life—and very settled in my ways!*
>
> ~ 51-year-old

We all hope for evolution in our lives, such as making choices and changes step-by-step or growing old with the ones we love. And sometimes our lives actually work that way. At other times revolution rules, and we are completely upended by circumstances. Through all of these experiences, we have found that both successes and failures can be defining moments, in our relationships as well as in other areas of our lives. More and more as we grow older, we realize that choices about our intimate relationships are some of the most important decisions we will make in the ongoing process of building the life we want.

Children

Single mothers, married mothers, lesbian mothers, working moms, stepmoms, stay-at-home moms, or grandma moms? How many kinds of mothers are there? Did we have children young? Were we forty when we started having kids? Did we adopt our children? Did we put a child up for adoption? Did we grow up poor or in an abusive home and vow we would never let that happen to our children? Have we lost a beloved child? Did we long for children and spent money and years trying to become pregnant? Did our children just sort of happen without any planning?

Has every woman thought about being a mother? Most likely, we have at least considered it, even if only for a split second, although some of us debated for years. Did we feel called to motherhood? If so, was the answer a quick and easy yes, so that we did whatever was necessary to make it happen? Some women may have wanted children but could not have them, while others were ambivalent and then did. If we did not find a spouse or partner but still wanted children, did we do it on our own? If we chose not to have children, are we content with that decision now, or do we still wonder? We live in a time in history when all of these questions and options are possible. There may be cultural, family, or personal expectations about having children, but more than at any other time, we are free to answer the question in our own way.

I was forty-five when I began my second marriage; my husband was fifty-six; we each had two grown children. We had about fifteen minutes to decide whether or not to have a child together. We decided to not. It was a good decision!

~ Pam F., 58-year-old

Will I be forgotten? I am a single, childless woman in her midforties. I have mementos and pictures from my past. Who will I pass these on to? Will my nephews or niece value them like I do? As I research my genealogy, who will know my history? Is this why I became a teacher? One of my second-grade students yesterday appeared to have a profound realization. She said, "I know why you became a teacher. You like to teach, and you teach us." I dared not laugh out loud and just responded with "Yes." As I reflect, my motivation to become a teacher is much more complex. Maybe I became a teacher because I have a great need to pass on something—knowledge, anecdotes, culture—as a mother would. I love to tell my students anecdotes of my life. With my class changing every year, at least I don't hear, "You already told us that story."

~ Paige T., 45-year-old

It is interesting to consider how many options there are for motherhood in the world today. Not so very long ago, women were expected to have their children while they were young. The biological clock was ticking by the time we hit our late twenties. Thirty was just too old to start a family. Forty years ago, a doctor might have recommended a therapeutic abortion to a woman who became pregnant in her late thirties. Now, some women do not even start their first or second families until they are forty. Imagine, for the first time in history women in their early forties, who had children very young, are now becoming grandmothers, and other women, also in their early forties, are just starting families. The women are the same age, and their children are a generation apart!

I fell in love with one of the most gorgeous men on the face of the earth, and he happened to be nine years younger than I am. So much comes with marrying a younger man, especially one that has never been married before or had any children of his own. I already had three children from a previous marriage, so in my mind, my family was complete. I was completely done with that phase of my life and ready to move on to the next. And then a miracle happened. After several miscarriages, today I sit in my two-year-old son's room playing trains, laughing, kissing boo-boos, potty training, putting him in time out, cleaning up his messes, and being used as his personal jungle gym. I have two beautiful girls in college and a wonderful teenage daughter at home. By the world's terms, I was supposed to be at a place in my life where my children were raised and out on their own, and enjoying all of my new found time. In my young mind, that translated into freedom! But as I sit here at the age of forty-four, this little boy is the definition of freedom. Freedom from grown-up stress. Freedom from drama. Freedom from heartache. His sweet eyes, precious face, and priceless laugh give me a glimpse into true freedom. He has no idea that he has been my rock when both of my parents passed. He has truly been the dose of joy my entire family needs on a daily basis. He is exactly what God knew we needed. I thought my family was complete; I was wrong, it wasn't. God's plan is more beautiful, perfect, and pure than I could have ever imagined it to be.

~ Sally D., 44-year-old

I told my daughter the other day, you are going to be twenty-nine, and you have yet to get married and give me grandchildren. I'm going to be an old grandma. Let's go. Get on it.

~ Lucinda L., 53-year-old

Because the physical possibilities of motherhood have so greatly expanded, many of us are finding ourselves in an interesting position. For those of us who had our babies young, our children are entering adolescence and adulthood before we hit the deep changes of late perimenopause and menopause. But many women who had children well into our thirties and forties, or who are raising grandchildren, find our changing hormones and our teens' changing hormones happening at the same time! This is a new occurrence in the dynamics of raising children: these two profoundly important life transitions happening simultaneously in a family. What does this complicated situation mean for us and our children? Our generation of Middlehood women will be the first to negotiate this in large numbers. How does a woman who has come to the natural changes of Middlehood, including perimenopause and menopause, find a way to be true to her evolution? At the same time, how can she be present and connected to her children who are going through the natural changes of their major transitions? It is kind of like being in two places at once—which, of course, we all need to learn to do!

It takes all of our creativity, patience, and love to struggle with our changing bodies and emotions (think sleepless nights and hot flashes) while we are going to soccer games, driving Mama's Taxi, getting ready for meetings and deadlines at work, arguing about curfews, trying to get someone else to wash the dishes and pick up stuff in the living room, checking on elderly parents, and still manage a date night with our partner or spouse. No wonder we sometimes think we are going crazy!

One of the hardest pieces is having some time to ourselves. Most grown-up women find it difficult to just plug in our earphones and ignore everyone else like our teens do, but a part of us would love to do that.

I have a son in high school and another in third grade. My method for finding me-time is going in the bedroom, locking the door, and saying, "Mommy needs a time out right now." That, of course, upsets my youngest child. Even my husband and oldest boy are thrown off by it. All of them will stand outside the door, knocking, "Mommy?" "Hey, Mom?" "Honey?"

~ Julie A., 43-year-old

Their sense of Mom is that she is always there, always available. And she is available most of the time, but sometimes she desperately needs to have an hour of peace and quiet. Many of us will laughingly admit that we have even gone in the bathroom, locked the door, and spent longer than we needed just so we could read.

There are no easy answers for any woman or any family. For sure, we need to take care of ourselves, eat healthy, rest, get exercise, and sleep as we can. Comparing notes with women friends in similar straits might get us some new ideas, but whatever the methods, just like our teens wearing their earphones, we need time to allow our changes to happen so that we do not go crazy, and neither do our families.

Empty Nest

Middlehood covers nearly a generation of time in our lives, and women in early Middlehood will be in a very different position than women at the end. For most of us past the age of forty-five, the decisions about whether to be a mother or not are done. As perimenopause advances, our options diminish, and unless we are grandmothers raising grandchildren, by the time we hit our fifties, we are moving past the stage of having young children around on a day-to-day basis. Now we are coping with the questions of who we are when nest building is done.

All through motherhood, we have found that each time our child hit a new developmental stage, so did we. We experienced a peculiar mixture of feelings: the thrill of watching a baby, then a child, grow and change, master new skills, and become more and more independent. But in the midst of our awe and excitement about who they are becoming, we also feel grief at giving up who they were. As one woman says, "I love my grown-up children, but I really miss my kids!"

I bought my daughter, Kate, a bike when she was eleven or twelve. Soon after, we took part in a twenty-mile CROP Hunger Walk/Run/Ride. It was a beautiful fall day as we rode through the country to a small church. As we rode, I realized that Kate had no idea how the gears worked, and wasn't experimenting—just riding. We stopped at the top of a hill, and she was breathing hard. It had taken a lot of energy to get up the hill in the gear she was using. I asked if she wanted me to show her how to make it easier, faster, and more fun. Of course she did. I explained how the gears worked, and then with no demonstration, she nodded that she understood and took off. I never saw her again the whole ride—not even from a distance. When I got to the church, she was sprawled out on the front lawn with other riders, waiting for me. She was so proud—she'd done it by herself. She didn't need to ride with mom. She was fine. I will never forget . . . teaching her and then watching her ride away . . . by herself . . . never looking back. That was a moment I'll never forget. I gave her the tools she needed to leave me, but it was a bittersweet moment when she actually did.

~ Martha C., 43-year-old

The conscious releasing of children into the world and their own keeping is a delicate and crucial process. We will often be surprised, as Martha was that all Kate needed was a little information and she was ready to go. Think of Sandra and Reneé on Mount Kilimanjaro. We all recognize this moment from Kate and Reneé's point of view. Every one of us has left the ones who raised us, and we know the feelings of fear, hope, and exhilaration that come with growing up and taking our place in the adult world.

Now we are the ones in Sandra's place, having come to a stopping point where we are called to the courage of letting go. It is our turn to say, "This is as far as I go, but you go on. Go all the way if you can." Not all of us had parents who knew how or were able to take these steps with us in a good way. Not all of us as parents have been able to negotiate this time with our children without making mistakes—two steps forward, one step back. It is a dance and some days are more graceful than others. We try, as our parents did, and little by little we all move forward, learning to embrace what is fading and what is growing.

When I first read the story of Reneé and Sandra's climb up Mount Kilimanjaro a few years ago, I closely identified with Reneé. Although closer in age to Sandra, I identified with the youth and vitality that could make the trip, however difficult, to the top of Mount Kilimanjaro. Now with young adult children, I am, suddenly and completely, Sandra. We start off the great journey of parenthood strong and confident. Our children see us first as superheroes, and then as invincible and indestructible, and we need to be. We plan the trip up the mountain together, begin and walk along at the same pace for quite a while. Then, we, as parents, begin to slow. Our mountaintop is much closer for us than is our children's. And yet, this is what it is all for, to bring our children to the base of their adult mountains and send them on. We hope and pray they will make it, but we don't know for sure if they will. We want to grab our babies and carry them safely up their mountains, but we can't—they have to go on without us. We hope that we have taught them enough, and that no matter how difficult the climb, our children will make it successfully. I can see myself standing there with all my mixed emotions, bravely sending my children on and thinking at the same time, "But I want to go on. I want to climb that mountain!" And then, "Did I teach them enough, prepare them enough? Will they make it without me? Do I want them to? Am I ready to let go?" Sandra knew there was no way for her to continue. They were at the diverging path, and she would take, perhaps, the more difficult path down the mountain.

I think I know how she might have felt—no longer was she the indestructible, invincible, superhero parent, but a human woman, who loved her child enough to send her on. She must have been scared, not only of how ill she felt, but also of the realization that she was no longer who she thought she was. She had to become someone new in her daughter's life and her own. I understand exactly.

~ Polly T., 57-year-old

Is it easy to let go? No way! Do we feel sadness, fear, relief, and hope all mixed together? Absolutely! Some days we want to hang on, tempted by fond memories of the past, or with panicky feelings that we have not taught them everything they need to know. Other days, we cannot wait for them to move along, to just get out there and do things for themselves.

I have great relationships with my children currently. In the past, I had many challenges with my daughter, who tends to make bad choices and thrives on drama and chaos. But I was careful not to burn bridges and, luckily, so was she. And luckily she lives two thousand miles away.

~ Judy K., 61-year-old

All of us will grapple with some feelings of sadness as we say good-bye to our children's childhoods. No matter how proud and excited we are for them, we feel the deep change that comes as they enter adulthood and begin to make lives and choices without us. For those of us who are alone, that good-bye may be even more complicated. Not only will we have an empty nest, but we will also have an empty house, and the sadness may include profound loneliness.

We have always given our children the best we had to offer, but now the story changes focus from what is good for them to figuring out what is good for us. The best part of our nests emptying is that we can pull our focus back from our children and put it on ourselves again. The worst part of our nests emptying is that we have to pull our focus back from our children and put it on ourselves again!

Most of us feel a bit lost and confused when the day-to-day work of raising children is done or changes dramatically. What does it mean when we have been building a home for a long time, and suddenly nobody really seems to need that home anymore? At the very least, it means fewer distractions and less commotion and clutter underfoot! On a deeper level, it may also mean emotional changes, like trying to sense our child's feelings long distance or learning to be a sounding board without offering solutions. On very deep levels, if we are women who felt a profound call to motherhood and knew it to be one of our purposes in life, then we may need to spend time finding new meaning in our lives. This is certainly a time of changes, large and small, and we may be surprised at the range of emotions we encounter.

The three steps of the Equation for Transformation could be very useful to help us sort out where we are in the process of letting go and starting a new phase. As always, we have to start with releasing our grip on how things used to be. There may be new work ahead or grandchildren down the line. There are many new possibilities, but they are in the future. The first step is letting go of what is completed and owning all of the feelings that go with it. What we need most now might be some quiet time and rest, followed by good conversation with our partner or spouse and other people we love.

Despite the fact that we are still busy with work, activities, helping our parents, or seeing friends, a real space has opened up inside us, and it is filled with questions. The particular questions may vary, but most of them, at the source, are about who we are and what we love to do. We may wonder about the qualities we have that make us good at being mothers and what we loved best about raising children. We may revisit childhood or adolescent dreams and pick up threads from our past. As we answer some of these questions, we will gain insights about our qualities that will always remain with us.

It may not take long before we start to say, "What now?" If we have been working mothers, juggling family and career, we might find that we can finally relax a bit. Others may be looking forward to starting back to work or devoting more time to building a career. For many of us, a creative answer might be to try something different, explore a part of ourselves that we have never developed before. Our new ideas could be as simple as having more time to be active, read, or just find more space for ourselves.

Launching our children is not easy for any of us; it is even more complicated when we have children with disabilities. They may not be able to live independently right now, or ever, and we will have to make arrangements for them. Even so, we must find new ways to assist ourselves so that we can grow as we need to and still be able to love and care for our children.

My husband and I never really thought that much about having an empty nest, because our oldest is mentally disabled. We have just accepted the fact that he may be with us for a long time. He may have an opportunity to move in with someone. These opportunities have come up, but he's been not ready or scared. It may not come up, so . . . I do treasure the moments when my husband and I are alone in the house. We don't have many intimate moments, but we've kind of gotten used to having my adult son around. You get used to it, but there are times when I wish I had more alone time.

~ Carol S., 50-year-old

Our love and concern for our children will never end, but trying to figure out what is best and how to help them at this juncture can be confusing. Should we give them money or a car or a down payment? Should we use our influence or connections to help them get a job? Where exactly is the line that marks their independence and our assistance? One of the classic questions is, what happens when we are trying to have empty nests and just cannot seem to get the baby birds to take off, or if they do, they come back again? This outcome is more likely in a bad economy, when our adult children still need help financially, but it brings up many issues about where we are as we transit this life passage.

> *Every time my daughter has needed to move back home because of divorce or whatever crisis at the moment (and bringing her children with her), I feel like I'm repeating a chapter of my life that still has lessons to be learned. Are they my lessons or theirs? It's hard to turn away family when they are in crisis, but at what point do you say "enough?" I can't help but think I keep getting older . . . yet going backwards.*
>
> ~ Anne C., 59-year-old

The nest-building work of motherhood is temporary, and unless we have an adult child with disabilities, our children will eventually move on, and so will we. Once a mother, always a mother, that is guaranteed, but our lives are layered and complex. As much as we love being a mother, we are also more than that. It can be incredibly difficult to let go of this beloved time of life, but we need to do something so we do not get stuck and miss out on the next creative cycle of our lives.

Our couple relationship may also undergo some significant changes. Are we looking forward to spending more time together, or are we feeling anxious about the loss of distractions and shared activities that we had because of the children? Do we hope to revitalize our relationship with our spouse or partner? For sure, we will need to bring honesty and compassion to our conversations about our future lives together. This is a big change for both of us!

> *I kind of dreaded the empty nest thing, and then in another way, I really looked forward to it. I think when it came close and our youngest was ready to go, my husband and I just looked at each other and said, "Well, we can just be happy about this, start having some fun and do what we want to do, or we can just be down in the dumps." We decided we would just have fun with it. And it was an easy transition. We enjoyed each other so much more than we had in years. We started having fun, having date nights, which didn't exist since we had kids. . . . We really learned to enjoy each other's company again.*
>
> ~ Jan S., 55-year-old

Once we have found peace with the changes of this time and are ready to look to the future, we could have fun playing with other kinds of questions, ones that can help us create imaginative possibilities. For example, as we gain clarity on why we love being mothers, we might start to wonder what is in our lives now that we can help birth. Is there a new idea or talent that could benefit from our assistance? What could we help nurture? Are there young organizations or people who could use the enthusiasm and perspective that we can offer? We will not be doing the work as we did in the past. Those days are gone, but there is so much we can do if we take the talents and experiences we have accumulated and use them in new ways.

Reflection Questions

- Are my intimate relationships only a reflection of who I was a long time ago, or do they still hold true for who I am becoming? What do I want in a relationship right now?
- Am I alone and happy with my life? What makes that possible?
- How are my relationships with my (nearly) grown children? What would help them and me grow into new understandings?
- How am I filling the space that has opened up as my nest empties?

CHAPTER 8

The Ones We Love: Parents, Siblings, Grandchildren, Relatives, Friends

Love is a force more formidable than any other. It is invisible—it cannot be seen or measured, yet it is powerful enough to transform you in a moment, and offer you more joy than any material possession could.

> ~ Barbara de Angelis, *Chicken Soup
> for the Couple's Soul: Inspirational Stories
> About Love and Relationship*

The woman dear to herself lives in the heart, alive to the everywhere presence of divinity. The woman dear to herself does not lose herself in the presence of man, woman, or child.

> ~ Mohja Kahf, *E-mails from Scheherazad*

ONE OF THE STRENGTHS AND CHALLENGES of Middlehood is our growing awareness of how much time we have—before our children are grown and gone, before we retire, before our parents can no longer care for themselves. This new ability to see ends coming is a powerful tool in developing priorities, but it can also create confusion and frustration. How do we decide who is most important at any given moment. Our parents?

Our kids? Where is time for our friends? And where is time for
us? We are filled with questions that have no obvious answers
and difficult situations that have no perfect solutions. But
Middlehood women know how to love, and love we will through
the challenges and confusion. Whether it is parents, children,
other family, or friends, we will love wholeheartedly, as best
we can, always.

Parents

Our parents. At different times in our lives, we loved them
unconditionally or hated their rules and regulations. We desperately
wanted to be like them or swore we never would be. We cringed
every time they said, "You'll thank me for this someday," or "Think
of all the starving children in . . ." when we did not want to eat
our peas. And exactly how old were we the first time we heard our
mother's words coming out of our own mouths?

What kind of parents did we have? Were they loving? Funny?
Quiet? Loud? Absent? Artistic? Workaholic? Alcoholic? Dreamers?
Abusive? Strict? Depressed? Church-going? Could they sing and
dance? Build things? Did they love to paint anything that didn't
move? Work hard? Play in a band? Were they different races or
religions? Did they speak English? Were they gay or bisexual?
Adoptive? Foster? Step? Divorced? Widowed? Who are these people
who raised us?

*My mom was a very strong and independent woman
and stood on her own. When things got tough, she got
tough. When the money wasn't there because my dad was
learning how to fly and all the money went towards flying
lessons, it was popcorn and hot chocolate for dinner on
Fridays. It was a fun time because Mom made it fun and
we played games. . . . We didn't realize that we were having
hot chocolate and popcorn for dinner because that was all*

we had in the house. It was a special treat and we looked
so forward to it. She did those things for the three of us
girls.

~ Jan S., 55-year-old

Regardless of our circumstances, all of us have a lot to learn about our parents. When we were growing up, we did not know them as people; we saw them only through the narrow lens of what we wanted and how they treated us. We had no idea about their fears and dreams or what it took to raise their children, trying not to make the same mistakes as their parents.

Like sun and air, our parents are simply in our lives until the day they leave us. It does not matter whether we get along or are estranged. It does not matter whether we live near or far from them. They gave us life, and until they are gone, we cannot imagine the world without them. For some of us, that day of reimagining the world came far sooner than for others. If our parents died before they were old, then we miss them with an extra layer of loss; we miss the opportunity to ask them questions about all the parts of our lives that are still to come.

I was orphaned at age forty-three. Some people have said
that that's not a valid use of the word . . . doesn't "orphan"
imply "child?" No. That is definitely the right word, and
that is definitely what I felt. And even with the difficult
situations of an aging, failing parent, and the care-giving
decisions and burdens that I know so many have . . . I
often envy people who have one or both parents, still.

~ Pam F., 58-year-old

If we are lucky enough to still have our parents here in Middlehood, we may find that many things in our relationship begin to change, and we might be surprised at how fast and deeply those changes begin to happen. For instance, we could suddenly recognize that our parents will always worry about us, and the worry is their love and concern. That realization could make a big difference in how we respond to what used to irritate us in the past.

> *I'm over at a friend's house, and we are going out to dinner, and her mother is visiting. We are walking out of the house, and her mother says, "Becky, don't forget to take a sweater!" She looks at me and says, "I'm still twelve to her."*
>
> ~ Lucinda L., 53-year-old

When we spend time with our parents these days, we learn new things about them all the time. Now that they are relieved of the responsibility of making sure we turn out right, they can show us who they really are. We have a chance to see them in new ways. If our relationship with our parents was troubled, maybe we can find forgiveness and understanding now—a profound healing for all of us.

We may have been fortunate to come from families that kept old family stories alive. But for many of us, all that family history they wanted to share was too old-fashioned, even boring. Now we have to catch up, because who we are has a lot to do with where we came from.

> *I love my mom's stories about being a college student in Europe right after World War II. Some of them are really funny. She laughs so hard while she's telling them that we start laughing too and almost miss the punch line!*
>
> ~ 50-year-old

After my dad's Parkinson's started to get bad, I went with him to visit his oldest friend. I'll never forget how Bob trimmed my dad's fingernails. He was so gentle, so tender. I almost cried to see how much this guy loved my dad. They'd been friends for sixty years!

~ Jane T., 45-year-old

Recently, I started going to lunch with my mom and her friends at their Ladies Luncheon, as they call it. It is really fun! She is so funny and her friends are wonderful.

~ 42-year-old

My father's family was from Lebanon. When he was young, he and his brothers and sisters spoke some Arabic. He forgot most of it as he grew up, but in his eighties, he started to remember words and phrases. I was very interested and asked him to teach me. One of the Arabic phrases he taught me was "Allah Maik (God be with you)." After that, we never ended a conversation or left each other without saying it.

~ Nancy G., 54-year-old

If we are going to do the work of the Equation for Transformation in our lives, we need to know what we should embrace and what we should let go. For instance, many of us know that a "family curse" is a very real thing—whether it is a gene for a physical weakness; a learned family pattern of anger, abuse or addiction; or a misery-producing fear of love and intimacy. We need to know how we got here, and our parents hold the key to some of that information in their stories about themselves.

Why is it important to understand our parents and family history? Because when we open up our awareness and listen as the stories begin to flow, we can start to trace patterns in them and in ourselves. Who was brave? Compassionate? Adventurous? Who shamed, blamed, or praised? Who passed on feelings of value, worthlessness, or control? This knowledge can help us understand our own strengths and fears, as well as the health and happiness of our relationships with other people in our families.

If we are committed to healing and growing, if we want to pass on the best of who we are to our children and the world, we have to know the truth. No games, no disguises. The Equation for Transformation requires honesty and fearlessness. Just like with our adolescent children, we are in a massive life change at the same time as our parents are: we are working our way through Middlehood, and they are working their way through elderhood. It is a natural place for reflection for both of us. As they enter the last phase of life, they are remembering and considering their lives: choices, regrets, what they did and did not do. Why is this important for our own growth? Because the more we can release and heal what is still painful between us, the more easily we can join them on this final part of their journey.

Not all of us are able or want to do this work with our parents, but those of us who can will find a real gift. We could grow much closer. If our parents were gentle, they might become even more loving; an angry parent might become softer; a cold or distant parent might begin to open up. As we begin to see them as complex people, not just "Mom and Dad," they see us not just as grown-up kids, but as skilled, knowledgeable adults. It can set all of us free—free from old fears of judgment, disapproval, and family patterns—and open up new possibilities for our relationship, appreciation, and growth.

My parents finally started to let go of their expectations and began to see me. I never wanted to go to college, and my dad never understood that. I always felt like I'd failed him somehow. Then one afternoon when I was in my early forties, my dad said, "I know you didn't go to college, but it's kind of like you have a Ph.D. in life." For the first time, I felt like he saw me, and I'll never forget that as long as I live.

~ 48-year-old

These times with our parents are precious, moments that we will value long after they are gone.

When my Momma was eighty years old, and I went to visit her, we would spend late evenings and many times into the early morning talking about her life with Papa, her twelve children, thirty grandchildren, and how they all turned out. She would often say she wished she were sixty years old again, because she loved that time in her life. Those precious late-night chats will be something I will remember forever, because it was in the quiet of the night that she really opened up to me and gave me the incredible gift of herself.

~ Nancy G., 52-year-old

In the early part of our Middlehood relationship with our parents, we hope they are enjoying themselves and their retirement. It is easy to find fun ways to be together, whether at family events, on vacations, or on projects. But as years go by, our relationship with our parents changes again. Now when we visit, we more likely help with chores and activities. Maybe we first do physical chores: cleaning the gutters, painting the spare room, or trimming the bushes. We are glad to help, and maybe even like the feeling of a different kind of responsibility with them. It seems natural: we are younger and stronger, so why not?

It is always hard for me when I first arrive home to see my mother and father. I come whirling in—racing at high speed, talking too fast, jumping up to do chores, planning too many activities. My folks just sort of watch me in quiet astonishment. Then as the hours and days pass, I start to slow down. I relax into their speed of life. I sleep later, enjoy quiet afternoons on the porch, and start to listen more and talk less.

~ 43-year-old

As time goes by, we find ourselves stepping in to help in other ways. We start to answer questions, do internet research, or make calls about insurance, medical procedures, and finances. Slowly, the ways in which we are needed become more numerous and more personal. At first we help with small things, even though they feel big at the time, like moving the holiday dinner to somebody else's house. Changing everything from the way it has always been is jarring. But sooner or later, we understand that Mom does not have the strength to clean and cook and host the family gathering anymore. And we really do need to take the children home after a couple of hours, because Dad needs a nap. As hard as those changes are, they are nothing compared to the ones that are coming for many of us and our parents as they get older. If we have the privilege and opportunity to care for beloved parents in the final stages of their lives, we will find unexpected challenges and whole new levels of love.

No one could tell you how hard it is to have parents who are aging—losing their own independence and having to depend on their children. Our parents have two different issues. My parents are financially stable, but my stepfather of thirty years died last year. He and my mom were in Arizona, so I could not be right there with her. That was hard. Now I see my mom dealing with being lonely. She has many friends and is very active, but I can tell there are still many times she is home alone for too long at a time. I try to call her, and have to deal with guilt when I get too busy. I need to balance that with my marriage, and with my children and grandchildren and making time for them. The best thing we have done during the summer is to have my mom and our daughter with her husband and children over for dinner one night a week. We have three generations—my mom eats better without having to cook and gets to spend time with her grandchildren and great grandchildren. I have really enjoyed these dinners also, and it has helped the guilt. No matter what the hard things are, there is plenty of love and laughter to share that keeps us all together.

~ Lynn T., 50-year-old

We know our parents are slowing down, but we still think things are relatively okay—until something happens, and we realize that we do not really know what is going on with them. We may not be getting the full story. Some of our first concerns might be about their medications. Are they taking them? What if they don't want to? What are the side effects? Money could become a concern. Are they paying their bills on time? Can they afford their medicine? Then we may begin to worry about their safety. Have they fallen? How independent are they—really?

My mother was so worried about money that she would fill her prescriptions and then cut all the pills in half to make them last longer. No wonder her blood pressure wouldn't stabilize!"

~ 49-year-old

My parents are from the generation that doesn't like to bother or upset anybody. When the doctor says, "How are you feeling?" my father will say, "Fine, thanks!" no matter how sick he is! I realized I needed to go to all of his doctor appointments with him.

~ 47-year-old

Some people may say that now we are parenting our parents, but that is not exactly the case. It would be so much easier if it were. Then we would know what to do and how to feel. We *are* doing things we never dreamed of, but nothing in the definition of a parent applies to us as we help our parents through the last part of their lives. Their growing limitations might require us to take over roles and tasks or make decisions for them, but we did not birth or raise them. We are simply caring for them.

My Papa had always done something he called "sharing." Out of the clear blue, he'd send a surprise check to all of us grown children for no particular reason. Unfortunately, his medical expenses had gotten so high that he and my Momma couldn't afford to do that anymore. He didn't realize that his savings were getting really depleted. I was the one who had to tell him he couldn't do it anymore, and he was really upset. But even though I couldn't let him do what he wanted to do, I had to remember he was a father and provider, trying to take care of his family—that's what was going on.

~ Nancy G., 57-year-old

Helping our parents take care of themselves is not the same as helping a child who does not know how. Our parents know perfectly well how to take care of themselves; they just cannot do it all anymore. The most difficult time is when they do not realize they need help, or they do things that put themselves or others in danger. Then we have to step in for their sakes and the sake of others.

Mom's driving got more and more erratic until nobody wanted to ride with her anymore. She thought she was still doing okay, but she wasn't. None of us wanted to tell her. It was so hard for her and us to accept—my mother was always the best driver in the world!

~ 53-year-old

My dad was always good with money—very thrifty and careful. It never occurred to us that he might not be able to handle his finances anymore until we found out that he had gotten caught in a telephone scam that preyed on seniors and had paid $5,000 for nothing! It took us months, with the help of the bank, the credit card company, and a lawyer, to get half the money back!

~ 61-year-old

To an outsider, it might seem relatively simple: just take the car keys away or take the checkbook home with us. So easy to say and so hard to do. There is nothing simple about this process with our parents. They do not want to feel dependent on others and, just like every one of us, they have their own relationship to money, control, and independence. Someone might ask, "Well, can't you just take over the finances for your dad?" They do not know how poor our father was growing up and how many obstacles he had to overcome to achieve financial success; that he expresses his love for his children by giving them money; that his image of himself as a man involves taking care of his family; and on and on. Sorting out these issues and finding workable solutions that allow our parents to retain dignity and choices is enormously complex.

My dad developed a dementia when he was in his seventies. His big thing had always been going to the bank to get some cash—he always wanted to have cash in his wallet in case he needed it. One day, two years after his driver's license expired, he drove himself to the bank. The bank called us because they were so concerned. He managed to get himself back to his assisted living facility but left the car in some far lot and had to walk through several buildings to get home. We realized after that how important it was to him. We'd only been thinking about taking care of him so he didn't have to worry about money. After that, we always made sure he had some cash in his wallet. Whenever we went out, we'd say, "Got your wallet, Dad?" He'd pull it out, check for cash, and then smile, "Yup!"

~ 49-year-old

Most of our parents have always worked hard, taken care of their families, and relied on strength and determination to get through hard times. They are proud of their self-reliance and cannot imagine a time when they can no longer take care of themselves. In fact, one of their biggest fears is being a burden, and they may not talk a lot about how they feel. If we try to put limits on them, even for their own safety, they will try to deflect us, or even sneak, in an effort to do something for themselves. And if they do get frustrated and lose their tempers, they are still not acting like children. They are acting like grown-ups who hate being dependent and are humiliated and embarrassed to have to ask for help.

Mom, she's hanging on as long as she can. Even though we're there, she's not giving up doing the bills, handling the money, still driving. She still feels like she can, because for her, as soon as we say, "no more," then she's done—she has nothing. Sure, she has children who love her and would do anything for her, but then she'd have nothing for herself.

~ 48-year-old

My mom was a lot younger than my dad, so she naturally assumed he would go before she did. She'd always had this dream of a little house all to herself. Unfortunately, by the time my dad died, my mom was having terrible memory problems, and there was no way she could live by herself. She did not want to hear that!

~ 56-year-old

Most of us resist these changes just as much as our parents do. It is painful to watch them lose their abilities and strength. It is easy to get impatient with them because of that pain and because our lives are so complicated with work, kids, and schedules. All of us want to do what we want to do when we want to do it. That is pretty simple, and much of helping our parents will fall in this category: when to shop, do chores, or make appointments. It takes patience—ours and our parents'—to negotiate all of this.

New questions come faster and faster as they get older. Is Mom safe in the shower—what if she falls? Do they need meals brought in or someone to cook for them? Do we need to turn the den into a bedroom for Daddy? When was the last time they took a shower or bath? Should we do laundry for them? What if Momma leaves the gas stove on? Is there a neighbor who can check on them? We print out phone lists, fill the refrigerator with food, carry loads of laundry back and forth, and always we worry. We are scared when the phone rings late at night or when we call them, and they do not answer. Over and over we worry, "What is going to happen?"

The truth is, things will get harder. Mother's memory loss and Daddy's lost balance will not come back. The questions and choices we face now are more difficult. Should we hire people to help when we cannot be there? Should they move in with us? Do they need assisted living, or can they stay in their own home?

Our long-distance society adds even more dimensions to the questions. If we live far away, every time we visit, we will be shocked by how much they have aged, and each time we leave, we will be seized with fear and anguish. If we live close, some days we will feel so overwhelmed trying to juggle our parents, children, families, and work that we may feel like we are on the edge of a breakdown. Then five minutes later, we will be wracked with guilt because we do not spend more time with our elder parents. If our parent lives with us, we may feel calmer and less worried but more exhausted because there is no retreat. There are no easy answers or shortcuts through this time, and every family story is both different and the same. We can only stay the course as best we can.

For many of us, realizing what end-of-life care for a loved one will involve is initiated by the shock we feel the first time we have to help a parent bathe or go to the bathroom. In this culture, needing help with these personal daily activities is the ultimate experience of helplessness and loss of control. It is wrenching, even frightening, and until the moment it happens, almost incomprehensible. What happens if our disabled father has to use the bathroom when we have taken him for an outing? Of course he will, and we will have to troop into the women's room together! If we think this is hard for us, imagine what it must be like for our dad.

I remember the first bath I gave my dad. That was a huge shock! I don't know if it was more embarrassing for him or for me, but I just remember we were waiting for the water to change, he thought it was too cold, and I kept saying, wait a minute . . . trying to make chitchat while he was buck naked. The longest awkward minute ever!

~ Peggy H., 54-year-old

Now is the time to put on our big girl clothes and step up. If we can let go of our discomfort and grace our parents with our patience, love, and respect, the difficult things get easier. After a while, they do not even matter anymore. When we can get to that point, we help our parents get there too. What really matters is not bathroom stuff—ultimately, that is utterly unimportant. What really matters is our parents' mind and spirit, personality, history, and core. Unless they have dementia or are in a coma, their most important attributes remain.

Perhaps our greatest gift to our parents at this point in their lives—and in ours—is to help them detach from what is not important. They will cling, like all people do, to images of themselves from the past, and they will continue to worry about things such as whether they look okay. They might need reassurance that their lives have been of value, that they were a good parent or spouse. Whatever we can give them in love and respect is what we should offer. We may surprise ourselves and find a well of love and patience we never knew we had.

And guaranteed our parents will surprise us. The quiet little woman who always bowed to the will of her dominant husband may exhibit strength, even stubbornness, later in life. The ambitious, hard-driving man we grew up with may have a soft side with his grandchildren that he never showed when younger. This time of life may very well open up new opportunities for us and our parents.

We have spent all of our lives watching our parents and learning from them. We are their beneficiaries not only of material things but also of the lessons they have taught us. Sometimes the lessons were positive, and we became generous, loving, skilled, and patient. Sometimes we learned clearly which qualities we did not want. Either way, this time is critical: we are in the process of building our futures and making vital decisions that will carry us into our own elderhood. Will we whine and complain? Be stoic?

Rage against the wrinkles and age-related losses? Find joy in new things? We are watching our parents, and our children are watching us. They will learn a lot from what we do and how we do it. What do we want them to see?

> *There is an old folktale about a man who became so old and weak that he could barely hold a spoon. He always made a mess when he tried to eat. His son and daughter-in-law were disgusted and put the old man behind the stove with a clay bowl so they didn't have to watch him. Before long, he was too weak to hold the clay bowl, and it fell and broke. His son and daughter-in-law were furious and gave him a cheap wooden bowl to use. Soon after, the old man's young grandchild was sitting on the floor, building something with small pieces of wood. When the father asked what it was, the child explained, "It's going to be a bowl for you and Mother to eat out of when I am big." The wife and husband looked at each other and began to cry. Then they went and got the grandfather and brought him back to the table.*

Being on this journey with our parents may be as difficult as it is joyous, but we *are* on this journey with them—for their sakes and for ours.

Siblings

Who really knows our history? Who was there through the family joys and struggles? Who remembers the old neighbor who taught us to whistle, the smell of our grandmother's barn, or our first cat or dog? Who knows about the time we almost got caught and had to hide for two hours? (Of course, we *never* told our parents this one!)

Except for our parents, no human beings on the planet have known us as long as our siblings. While our parents are around, we can still ask questions about the past. "How did that happen?" "What was I like?" "Why did we go there?" Those questions are easy to answer while our parents are still available to fill in the details. Once they are gone, however, only our siblings have a clue about where we came from and what we were like as children. Even our oldest friends and cousins do not share our entire early history. A sibling was in the family with us—in the house and in the stories. They hold our history with us because it is their history too. For most of us that sharing becomes precious at some point in our lives.

As we grow older and come into our middle years, we begin to see our siblings differently. No longer are they the older sister who never had time for us or the little brother who followed us everywhere. Now they are real grown-ups—people we can count on for help. Some of us have always been close to our siblings, seeing them as confidantes, guides, or friends. Some of our sibling relationships have been difficult or broken apart, and we do not know if we will ever mend them.

My brother and I were once the closest of friends; now we're bitter enemies. We have drawn our lines and taken up arms. Yet we are more alike than different—how we both struggled to be accepted and loved. How we both yearned to belong. I see that we were both victims of the past, trying for years to please those that rejected us. I want to say this to him: "We are no longer friends. But you are still my brother. No amount of pain or animosity can change that. In the end we are tied to each by our father's people. Once we were familia, once we were for each other, once we were unconditionally accepting of each other. To honor that time and the abuelos we both cared for, I send you love from afar. I am sorry for causing you pain. I forgive you for the pain you caused me. I am your sister always."

~ Renee F., 44-year-old

We may have lost our connections with siblings due to time and distance, and suddenly find ourselves missing them and wanting to be in touch. Even if we did not get along as children, we might understand each other much better now.

For many of us, the first impetus to refind or deepen our relationship with sisters and brothers begins as our parents' health and circumstances change. We have decisions to make together and need each other's help and insights. Or perhaps we, or our sibling, are having health problems. Sadly, like many people, we will often take steps to improve our relationships only when forced by difficult circumstances.

One of the dangers to our relationships with brothers and sisters at this time is the terrible stress we experience when our parents become disabled or ill. There are so many decisions to make and fears that arise. We worry about family finances and meeting our parents' wishes about end-of-life care. We have to find ways to share the responsibilities and costs of taking care of them. These negotiations are difficult for many families and can reveal deep differences in our ideas about what is right and good.

Even more than when we were young, now is the time to speak the truth as we know it, tell our siblings how we are feeling and what we need, and listen as they share their fears and feelings. It is possible for brothers and sisters to find a profoundly new and deeper connection through this process, gaining great respect for qualities that we did not know we had. Perhaps the baby sister is the person best equipped to take over finances or health decisions for our parents. Older siblings might feel confused as they try to release old ideas about who this sister is and let go of their own feelings of needing to be the "boss of everything." Maybe the quiet older brother is the one who shows up at the folks' house every day or every week to help with whatever needs doing. Did we even know that he had chosen to stay in our hometown to help our parents? What about the older sister who always seemed to be such a free spirit, with only distant connections to the family? Did she move back to help when things got complicated? And what about the ones who always stayed close? How are they feeling as the family dynamics shift and change? Do they feel a deepening of their relationship to their parents? Do they welcome the long-distance sibling to the inner circle?

My youngest sister was always the baby of the family. I was so used to looking out for her, that it never occurred to me that she might step up, in a big way, to take care of our parents when they were in the last year of their lives. When I visited, I got to see how smart and strong she was, handling all the details of their care and finances. I was so impressed with her. This was a whole part of her I had never seen before. I felt so grateful to have her there. I knew my parents were safe with her looking out for them.

~ 52-year-old

Now the adults we have come to be will be needed and will possibly surprise other members of the family. All families have a story or myth about each member, stories that we do not even question. Sometimes those stories are true—to a point—but mostly, they have become outdated as we have grown older. Now is the time for all of us to get to know each other in new ways.

Grandchildren

While we rebalance from changes with our parents and negotiate the early stages of empty nests, we might settle into a cycle in which our children are no longer our main focus. Our young adult children have lives and adventures of their own—and so do we! We will always love keeping up with their work, travels, and loves, but for now, our lives and theirs do not intersect nearly as much as they used to. We may find ourselves communicating more often by e-mail, text, or video chat than sit-down Sunday dinners.

And then for many of us, a new and mostly joyous stage begins: grandmotherhood!

> *Having our first grandchild has been such an amazing experience! Seeing that sweet little face brings back such wonderful memories of when our children were young. It's hard to believe how quickly time has gone by. It is strange to see our child raising her own small human. It just seems so unreal that we are entering the next phase of life where a new generation of our family has begun.*
>
> ~ Nan G., 44-year-old

This can happen sooner for some of us and later for others, but Middlehood grandmothers are a booming group. What an eye-opening experience: the return to changing diapers, babysitting, and chasing toddlers, with noticeably less speed and energy but just as much love.

> *I never knew, could not imagine.... I saw my new husband melt when his daughter gave birth to his first grandchildren (twins!); I beheld in wonder as my ex-Marine macho-outdoorsman big brother went completely mushy-gaga-nuts over his grandchildren; and of course every single time I walked into my husband's church, the secretary had to show me the latest pictures of her grandchildren I'd never met . . . still, I could not imagine. I met my first granddaughter when she was two days old and fell immediately, instantaneously, deeply crazy in love with her!!!! I had loved being a mom, enthusiastically mothered my children and practiced "attachment parenting," still love my grown sons more than language can describe . . . and I was not prepared for this!! People will talk about "biology"—which makes perfect sense to me*

*when talking about mother-love . . . but this generation-
removed grandmother-love is so mysterious to me and
beyond powerful! And it happened all over again with
Granddaughter #2! I'm a Happy Nana!*

~ Pam F., 58-year-old

Most of us light up and talk delightedly about how much
we love being grandmothers. We show pictures of our precious
grandbabies to anyone who expresses interest. We buy our favorite
picture books to read to them before they are even six months old.
And we cannot wait until they are old enough to go to the park or
the zoo, imagining all the fun to come.

It is painful for those of us who do not live close to our
grandchildren. We miss out on so many of the funny, astonishing,
and delightful things they do. We think about them all the time,
begging their parents for more photos and videos, counting the
days until the next visit or video chat or phone call. While they
are very young, we worry that they will forget us from one visit
to the next, and we melt into a puddle when they call us by name
and run to our arms as soon as they see us.

It really is all the fun of being a mom with so much less
responsibility. After all, spoiling our grandchildren is the point,
isn't it? And even better, we can just give them back to their
parents during a temper tantrum or the flu!

*I loved being a mother, and have always loved children, so I
knew I would love being a grandmother. I do, but it's much
different than I expected. I have the same joys—probably
more joys—being the grandma. I don't have to make sure
they get to the dentist or eat healthy, and it won't be my
responsibility to pick the right school, the right sport, etc.
I do get to make sure they feel loved, and I absolutely get
to enjoy spending time with them. When you are the mom,
you have laundry to do and the house to clean and dinner*

to make. When you are the grandma, those things can wait until the days when the boys are not visiting. I can focus on them and enjoy even the pouting and arguing. I think they are so smart and so cute. My grandson tells me he likes to come to our house because I do fun things with him. Pretty much the greatest feeling in the world.

~ Lynn T., 50-year-old

Some of us thought we would cruise into our golden years but suddenly find ourselves called upon to raise our grandchildren. This experience is quite different from babysitting or enjoying the children for a weekend or holiday. We did not plan our retirement finances to include the expenses of one or more children living with us for a decade or two. Watching for the best sales on school supplies was not what we thought would be important at this time in our lives. We are amazed at how much more exhausting it is to raise children now than when we were younger. Raising children is not what we thought we would do at this age, but we have lived long enough to know that life is full of surprises.

My daughter got addicted to alcohol and drugs and ended up in prison. At the time, she was raising two young children by herself. When she went to prison, the kids came to stay with me and my husband. We hadn't expected to be raising children in our late fifties—we thought those days were over. We sure don't have the energy we used to have, but kids keep you young! Some of it has been hard, emotionally and financially, and we can't even think about retiring any time soon, but really what else could we do? We love our grandkids and would do anything for them.

~ 60-year-old

The best we can do is to make our plans and then go along for the ride with what actually happens. We will rise to meet this challenge in the same way we have met challenges throughout our lives. We might need more help this time around, but we will give our grandchildren the best we have: our love, protection, wisdom and guidance. Then like all parents and grandparents, we will hope for the best.

Relatives (Aunts/Uncles/Cousins) and Other Special People

All of us may find ourselves reaching out to extended family as we travel through our Middlehood years. Some of us hunger to keep in touch with our pasts by connecting with our elder relatives or cousins, and if we are lucky, we still have family friends, godparents, or even birth parents we have found and gotten to know. Many precious people in our lives do not fit into any easy category, but we know they are important to our family. Maybe we were very close to an older woman who lived in our neighborhood when we were kids, and we still get holiday cards from her son. Maybe a man who played in the band with our father still stops by for a visit. Every family has an assortment of wonderful people who become more precious as we get older.

My father's family was small. Now that all of his generation is gone, my sisters and I find ourselves e-mailing and visiting our cousins a lot more. "There's so few of us left" is what we have begun to feel and say. It's like we have started to realize what we had and did not really appreciate when we were younger. Now we're making up for lost time.

~ 63-year-old

And it is not only people our age and older who have meaning for us. Even if we did not have children of our own, we might be powerfully drawn to young people in our extended family. We may develop a wonderful relationship with nieces and nephews, younger cousins, or our partner's or spouse's grandchildren.

> *My joys are that I can still sing and bring a smile or healing to another human. That is big. And being there for the young ones is important to me, whether nieces, nephews, grandchildren, or other children . . . being a rock for them brings me joy.*
>
> ~ Lauranne B., 46-year-old

Time and love are part of what makes people feel like family. For most of us the boundaries of family have stretched out many times in our lives and redefined the meaning of what a family can be.

Friends

Remember the old expression, "You can't choose your family, but you can choose your friends"? We were not very choosy when we were little; we played with any kids we encountered—cousins, neighbor kids, the kids of our parents' friends, kids we met at the playground—and they were all our friends if only for an hour or an afternoon. After we started school, we became more discriminating. We liked and did not like other kids because of how they acted, how they looked, or how popular they were. We were best friends with boys and girls until the boys were embarrassed to be friends with us anymore.

No matter how we looked or how much money we had, friendships were often a minefield in the journey of growing up. Many of us survived dreadful experiences, when it was hard to find a friend or when insecure girls with power tried to control our friendships. "You aren't my friend anymore!" "I won't be your friend if you're friends with *her*!" Remembering those awful, paralyzing moments when we were new at figuring out who we were can still induce a chill.

If we were lucky, we found some good, true friends early on. Remember how it felt to meet someone for the first time and feel like we had known them forever?

When I was in middle school and high school, I had a friend that I really liked. She never knew that my mom was an alcoholic and things at home were hard. She was kind and encouraging, and she always made me laugh! I wish I knew where she was now.

~ 54-year-old

Friends were often the center of our world when we were young adults. We remember living and traveling with our friends, helping each other through interviews, first dates, and moving. We partied, studied, shopped, and played sports. When we needed a date, a job or an apartment, we called each other. And always we talked—about our feelings, hopes, fears, and loves. We cried, we laughed, we worried and struggled. Whether or not we were dating, our friends were the sounding board as we pondered everything from the newest fashion to the meaning of life.

We are more of a sisterhood than other generations of women have been. We are okay with sharing our strengths and our weaknesses.

~ Lucinda L., 53-year-old

Many Middlehood women in our fifties and sixties made our friends part of our family, but we also took our friendships into the larger world. We encouraged each other in support groups and empowered each other in consciousness-raising groups. We formed local food co-ops and created community health clinics. Some of us pooled our money and started businesses or bought land and lived and farmed together. We may also have been part of caretaking circles for sick and dying friends. In many ways, large and small, we learned how to make communities, from close intimate circles of best friends to movements that altered our society in politics, health, education, arts, and business.

> *I have three "lifers," close friends I depend on for support, advice, and strength. I don't know what I would do without them. I have always had close women friends throughout my life.*
>
> ~ Linda S., 57-year-old

There are many legacies from those early years but also many changes. Few of us still travel around in herds like we used to, but many of us are still rejuvenated with a girls' night out. There really is nothing like a group of women friends to touch a place deep in our hearts, full of laughter and love and deep understanding.

> *I didn't have many friends as a kid, not until I got older. I met my oldest friend, Anita, when we were young adults just getting out on our own, and we had lots of adventures. After we both got married and had kids, we weren't in contact as much anymore, but whenever we were, it didn't matter how long it had been, it was like no time had passed. When I got sick, she was the first person I called. I'm also still friends with people I met when my daughter was in high school. Some of them I know I could call any time of day or night, and they'd be over here in a flash. When I was first sick and starting chemo, it almost felt like they were fighting over who was going to take me or pick me up from the doctor's. One day two of them showed up at my door with their cleaning equipment. I sat in the recliner*

and fell sound asleep while they cleaned my whole house! And even though I've been gone from my job for most of a year, I'm still friends with people from there. Usually a few months after you leave a job, it's like you don't have anything in common with them anymore. It makes me feel very special that they remember me and still want to be friends. Through my life, as I became more comfortable and had more confidence in myself, it was easier to make friends and like people. In order to like someone, you have to like yourself. People who are comfortable to be themselves around others often have lots of friends.

~ Helen M., 60-year-old

And our men friends—what about our men friends? Our men friends may have helped us navigate many confusing times as we grew up and sorted out our identities, interests, and relationships. Gay or straight, they have always had a perspective different from our women friends and provided insights we could not find elsewhere. No doubt they have needed us as well, grateful for the wider view that a woman could give them. We may not have had as many long and deep friendships with men as we have with women, but those that have lasted over the years are a real gift.

We are looking for the truth and the treasure in all of our relationships these days, and our friendships are no exceptions. We know the value of our old friends but still, we often struggle to find the time and energy to spend with them. Although we really like many people we work with or meet, we may hesitate to add someone new to our lives because we know it will take more of our precious energy.

I feel like my friendships are like building with Legos. There are only so many spots to fill. We are all running on full now, so for something to come onto my plate in terms of a new friendship, a new relationship, or a new anything,

*that means something has to come off my Lego. It's energy,
it's time. I don't have time for high-maintenance, low-
energy, nonfulfilling relationships anymore. I've got a lot
of years in front of me and I'm not wasting them with the
likes of somebody who is not fulfilling me.*

~ Lucinda L., 53-year-old

Because Middlehood is a long period in our lives, we are often
in vastly different places with our friendships. The primary reason
for those differences may depend on whether we have children
and how old they are. When our children are young, it takes
huge amounts of energy to keep up with everything. If we are
single mothers, our friends may be vital in our lives as long as
they can join us and our children in our home or activities. A
single mom has no built-in babysitter when friends want to go
out without the children. Stay-at-home moms often suffer from
"adult deficit disorder" and will strike up a conversation with
anybody just to have some grown-up conversation! For many of
us shared activities and convenience are pieces of the friendship
puzzle during this time in our lives. Can we mix together a play
date and a good visit? Can we meet after work for a quick drink
and conversation? Can we squeeze in some laughter and sharing
during the soccer game?

If our children are grown or nearly so, or if we have no children,
do we struggle with managing our friendships because we are
swamped with work? Caring for our aging parents? Are we losing
touch with old friends? Finding each other again on social media?
It is complicated, for sure.

*I don't have a great many friends, but those I do have are
very close. I look for friendships that are unconditional—
that they accept me for what I am and not try to change
me or judge me. They are supportive and they are there for*

me whenever I need them. I trust them to act in my best interest at all times.

~ Donna S., 55-year-old

Here are a few things that women say about their friendships now:

I have longtime friends, even lifetime friends, but I don't have daily friendships the way I used to. Sometimes I'm lonely for the way I used to do things with friends regularly.

~ Cindy L., 49-year-old

I have many close friends. Many since elementary/high school days. I look for someone who doesn't keep score on our relationship.

~ Dana G., 41-year-old

My girlfriends have been there with me, and will likely be there when I need to be talked off the latest cliff. My girlfriends have proven their value with long, tearful phone calls, drinks, and time. This weekend's date is a stranger at this point. He hasn't earned the right to trump my friends.

~ Sondra S., 55-year-old

My old friends help me remember my past. They remind me of what's always been important to me and, sometimes they remind me of how I've changed.

~ 60-year-old

I can just let go and laugh my ass off with my friends. That feels so good!

~ 49-year-old

When I was young, I used to wonder about all the Christmas letters my mom would write every year. I understood about the relatives, but who were all these "friends" we never saw? I thought friends were people you hung out and did things with, but she wrote to people she hadn't seen in twenty-five years! Now, I understand.

~ 58-year-old

No matter how old we are, most of us are powerfully aware of how important our friends have always been. Whether they provide a shoulder to cry on, help with childcare, a tampon at a critical moment, or assistance with everything when there has been a death in the family, they are people we rely on—part of the loving community that makes our lives work. Some friends are part of a certain segment of our lives, giving meaning, laughter, and love in a place and time, but they do not travel through the rest of our lives with us. If we have lost touch with our longtime friends, we may find ourselves hungry for connections of heart and spirit that only they can provide. As we continue through Middlehood and on, we may find that our friends reassume a central place in our lives. Sooner or later, our parents will pass on, work will slow down, children will grow up, and we will find ourselves with time and interests to share with friends again. It might be gray-haired ladies night out, but it will be just as funny, just as loving, and just as full of knowing and understanding as ever.

I have several close friends. I look for an ease of companionship and laughter. And those women I have known since our children were small offer a very special quality to our friendship. We needed each other so much back then, saw each other through many storms, and now ease each other into old age.

~ Gaye S., 63-year-old

A couple of the things that help me flourish at this age are my long standing support network of friends and the ceremonies I help plan for my birthdays. One of my favorite things to do is write spoofs of Broadway musicals. When I turned 60, a friend wrote and I sang, a spoof of "You're not dead yet" from Spamalot called, "You're not old yet!" Then we did a sing-a-long about menopause. After that everyone went around the room and shared how long they had known me, and what knowing me had given them. It was so moving and wonderful that I still get warm thinking about it."

~ Olivia M-S, 65-year-old

The heart of a Middlehood woman has loved many times, in many ways over the years. We have loved passionately, tenderly, thoughtfully, carelessly, and cautiously. We have had our hearts broken, and we have been profoundly surprised to have our hearts broken open. We have learned many of our biggest life lessons through our relationships and find ourselves filled with both regrets and profound gratitude. Are we done loving? No way, not by a long shot.

Reflection Questions

- How are my relationships with my parents changing? What helps us maintain trust and respect for each other through these changes?

- In what ways are my relationships with my siblings changing?
- What do friends mean to me at this time in my life? How is it different from when I was younger?

CHAPTER 9

The Passing of Parents and Other Good-Byes

Every great loss demands that we choose life again...
Grieving is not about forgetting. Grieving allows us
to heal, to remember with love rather than pain. It is a
sorting process. One by one you let go of the things that
are gone, and you mourn them. One by one you take hold
of the things that have become a part of who you are and
build again.

> ~ Rachel Naomi Remen, *My Grandfather's*
> *Blessings: Stories of Strength, Refuge*
> *and Belonging*

Before you know kindness as the deepest thing inside, you
must know sorrow as the other deepest thing.

> ~ Naomi Shihab Nye, *Words Under the Words*

WHEN EXACTLY DID WE BECOME ADULTS? When we turned twenty-one?
Had a child? Bought a house? Finished college? Got married? We
laugh now to think of how anxious we were as children to grow
up, to become adults with all the freedom we thought they had.
Imagine having money to buy candy whenever we wanted, to stay
up as late as we wished with no one to tell us to go to bed! Now
we chuckle with that remembrance or sigh with nostalgia for what
we gave up: the innocence, the joyful abandon of time and worries,

163

and the endless hopes of "tomorrow" and "someday." For every passage, the old way must die for the new to be born, so we gave up unlimited candy for a lifetime of teeth and late-night television for productive workdays. We let go of various options and possibilities for choices of depth and priority. We sacrificed ignorant innocence for knowledgeable hope.

In Middlehood we are giving up another piece of youthful innocence. When we were younger, most of us were shocked when someone we knew died. Now lots of us have lost one or both parents, and many of us, other people we love. If we ever had a romantic idea of death, it is gone now. We no longer believe that we are invulnerable and that death is for someone else—not for us and our loved ones. As J. K. Rowling's Harry Potter learns, certain things become visible only when you have seen death. This awareness may be the surest sign of the passage into Middlehood.

Time and experience are the teachers here. We learn the lessons because we have lived through them and felt what happens. Most of us would much rather read about it in a book, but the real stuff of life is made up of these experiences. They are the moments that change us forever, that irrevocably alter our ideas about death—and life.

Medicine by Jane Treat

My friend Elizabeth was a survivor of many traumatic events, most recently a very serious accident. She used a wide variety of healing methods to help her recover from those injuries. Some of those methods were primarily physical, others more spiritual, but all together they seemed to have a big effect. Those of us who loved her watched with amazement as her spirit seemed to grow larger and larger. Although she had always been strong, it seemed that more than just her body was healing.

And then she was diagnosed with cancer.

She went through numerous treatments, even surgery, but nothing seemed to help for long.

Early that spring, I was due to leave on a month-long trip to the rain forest in Mexico, and I was worried about being gone for so long. On my last visit before I left, Elizabeth read my mood as I was reluctantly getting ready to go.

"Jane, I'm glad you're going on this trip. I'll still be here when you get back." She smiled, her eyes twinkling.

I frowned.

"No, Jane, don't you see?" She spoke with sudden strength. "You know I love to travel, and I can't do it anymore. You have to go so you can come back and tell me about everything you do and see."

She meant it; I could see it in her eyes. I smiled and rubbed her fuzzy, nearly bald head. "You wouldn't rather have me lugging you to the doctor and baking potatoes?"

"No—you go. Be my eyes and ears."

"Okay, I'll come back with lots of stories," I agreed, trying to sound cheerful. "You want me to bring you something?" I tossed out the last line as I headed for the door, thinking maybe she'd like a weaving or piece of pottery.

She hugged me good-bye in the doorway, then pulled back, leaving her hands on my shoulders. "Yes." She looked me in the eyes. "Bring me some medicine."

I sucked in a breath of air as I nodded, thinking of her Native ancestry. After a moment, she nodded too, convinced I understood—not medicine for her body, but spirit medicine. Another quick hug and I left.

As I traveled through small towns and villages in central Mexico, I visited every market I could, looking for something that might be medicine. I found some copal, a fragrant tree resin used as incense by curanderas in ceremonies and healings. Later, I bought a little leather pouch to keep it in. But nothing else seemed like medicine. After days of prowling through markets and shops, I gave up the idea that the medicine I was looking for could be purchased in a shop. Anxiously wondering where I would find it, I continued on my trip.

During a long hike through the rain forest, I pondered Elizabeth's request. I remembered an old story about the strength of a puma. One of the teachings of the story was that a puma never tried to hide from potential dangers in the world. Instead, from the moment it is born, a puma is taught to accept those dangers and face the inevitable threats of life. It learns to challenge and fight, accepting the knowledge of its death. And because of that knowledge, a puma does not hide—it is free to live.

Suddenly, I realized that something had happened to Elizabeth through her healing experiences. It felt like she had put away any kind of hiding and had fully stepped into her puma life, aware of her frailties but full of courage and a passion for life. It was a powerful choice, and it profoundly affected all of us who knew her.

After many fascinating days in the rain forest, we returned to the village of our guide, Kin Bor. While we were there, Kin Bor gave me a jaguar tooth, and I knew that finally I had found the medicine for Elizabeth. Jaguar tooth— puma tooth—close enough! Delighted, I left Kin Bor's house clutching my jaguar tooth. I stopped to talk to Ignacio, a biologist traveling with us, and cheerfully showed him the tooth. He studied it very carefully, turning it over and over, peering closely. Finally, he handed the tooth back to me.

"I am most sorry to have to tell you this, but that is not a jaguar tooth."

"What! Are you sure?" I was stunned.

"Oh yes, it is very hard to see the difference, but these marks here—" he pointed to faint lines on the incisor, "not jaguar. Always, those marks are on the tooth of the puma."

Expecting disappointment, Ignacio was surprised by my reaction.

"A puma tooth! Yes! Perfect!" And off I went with the certainty that I'd found some medicine. I would put the tooth in the pouch with the copal and give it to Elizabeth along with the story of the puma.

The morning after I got home from Mexico, I called Elizabeth. After a quick hello, she blurted out, "Can you come over right now? I want you to help me with something."

As soon as I arrived, Elizabeth asked me to get a large photo album from the top shelf of her bookcase. We sat down on the couch to look at it. "I've been thinking about something all day. I don't know why I'm so obsessed with finding this picture, but I just can't stop thinking about it." Pictures of her childhood flew by as she flipped through the pages. At long last, she pointed to a picture. "There it is!"

I looked at an old faded photo of a creek. She pointed to a particular spot on the muddy hillside behind the creek, and I could just make out the opening to a small cave.

"When I was a little girl, that—" Elizabeth tapped on the picture, "was my hideout. Whenever things were hard at home, I'd run away and hide there. When I got older, I'd go to be alone and think. I always felt safe there." She paused. "That's so strange to me now when I think about it."

Elizabeth stared across the room for a few seconds and then turned her head and looked at me. I felt the skin on my upper back and neck start to prickle.

"A pair of pumas lived in that cave. I never saw them; they never came around while I was there. But why in the world did I feel so safe in a puma cave—even as a little girl!" She was quiet for a moment. "I haven't thought about that old cave in years, but today I just couldn't get it out of my mind. I had to see that picture."

I smiled, then opened my pack, took out the pouch, and gave Elizabeth her medicine. She quietly held the pouch as she listened to the story. Then she nodded, and breathed a simple, "Yes."

Elizabeth lived with courage, love, and a profound sense of wholeness for eight more months. The power of her choices did not cure her, but they did heal her from old fears and pain. And in her healing, Elizabeth helped all of us to heal. By the time she died, we had all chosen a new path. Like Elizabeth, we chose the way of the puma.

———

Most of us did not choose the way of the puma when we were young. Loving adults tried to protect us, tried to keep injury, harm, and loss far away. It makes sense to protect young ones, but even if we were very sheltered, losses happened. Maybe our favorite pet died. It was incomprehensible—surely s/he was just asleep and would wake up any moment. Or we had to move away from our best friends—how unfair! We learned about loss when our parents divorced or our favorite grandparent got sick and passed away. Ultimately, no one can protect us from loss and death. Life is the teacher, and the lesson is simple though not easy: death and loss are part of life.

Some of us had no gradual process of learning about death through goldfish or hamsters, cats or dogs. We jumped straight into the loss of a parent, sibling, or friend. With so little life experience to help us prepare, such a loss may have scared us into hiding to avoid ever feeling that terrible pain again. No doubt, it has taken a lot of living and loving to coax ourselves back out.

My mother's death affected me. She was diagnosed with cancer and gone within twenty-one months. While I am thankful the Lord prepared us and gave us time to say good-bye, I miss her terribly. She had incredible strength and will to live but knew when it came time that her good deeds on Earth were done and that the Lord needed her elsewhere. She was a pillar of strength for us all and was always worried about how everyone else was going to get along. I not only miss the time I will get to spend with her, but also the time my children will not get.

~ Dana G., 41-year-old

The Equation for Transformation is a clear and natural tool to use through the process of a loved one dying. The simple formula may come to our rescue many times, almost as a mantra: "Let go and make peace; wait and ponder; renew what remains and start again." We can feel the necessity to make peace with our fears, old anger, or resentments with the loved one, or the struggle with other family members, as we all try to sort out a lifetime of feelings and memories. When we are able to clear away what is old and jumbled, we may find we can be present to each other and the process, with fewer fears and judgments. In this clearer space, we are likely to discover moments of love and acceptance that are so much more than we ever imagined. And at some point, our loved one will go, and we will be left to find our way into a new chapter without them. If we have done the work of forgiveness and releasing, with patience and love, we will be better prepared, much more open to accepting the gifts and taking them with us.

It is important to understand where we are now because we have reached that time in life when we are beginning to absorb losses more frequently. The threads of these losses now weave through us—part of the tapestry of who we are. We will never live another moment without those threads, without that sadness, and we know there is more to come. Does this mean that we now live in a state of permanent depression? Are we afraid to love open-heartedly? Have we lost all joy in life? We may find ourselves in a dark hole for a while, but with love and time, we can see our options. Will we hide away from risk, love, and perceived dangers, or will we choose the way of the puma, accept death and loss as a fact of life, and choose to live fully anyway?

As we age, we face our mortality square in the face. In the last few years, I have lost a number of friends and family members to illness. Losing peers (or sometimes people even younger than yourself) makes you sit up and take notice that your life clock is slowly but surely running out of time. Although I have absolutely no fear of death, I do have a lot of living left to do and hope that I'm around long enough to get everything done that I want to do.

~ Donna S., 55-year-old

This is not the choice of a young person who doesn't really believe in death; here in Middlehood, we believe in death. Regardless of our religious or spiritual views on an afterlife, we understand that death means loss and change on a deep level. Our choice time comes because of this growing awareness that life here on Earth does not last forever. This simple awareness we have noted many times over the years now rings far more deeply. Its implications are enormous, because we have to decide what we are going to do with that knowledge. Will we pull back, hide out, grow more fearful? Or will we opt for the puma's way: love as deeply as we can, make every day count, and not waste time on unimportant things? Our choices now will affect everything about our lives for the decades to come.

This new awareness also changes our sense of priorities. If we start accepting death and loss as necessary realities, then we are going to give our attention to things that matter. What has real, lasting importance to us? Is it our house or car? Probably not. Is it our job? Maybe, if it is work that is important to us. Our religion or spiritual path? Very likely, if it is an honest expression of who we are. As we go down our list of valuables, most of us will find that it is not things we treasure, but people and experiences of wonder, insight, and mystery. Suddenly, accumulating things may seem much less important. Instead, spending time with people we love, actively doing something good in the world, having adventures and fulfilling long-held dreams may rise to the top of the to-do list. To find our way to the puma choice at this time in our lives is the beginning of real wisdom.

The Circle of Loved Ones and Caretakers

If we have not already, many of us will spend time with an elderly parent in the last weeks and months of their life in the not-so-distant future. We may also find ourselves companions and caretakers for younger people: family members or friends. It is a time of powerful and powerfully mixed emotions. We ricochet through denial, anger, fear, acceptance, hope, laughter, pity, love, and compassion. We want to be there; we do not want to be there. We want to help; we want to run away. It is an exhausting, precious time. Everything else in life recedes in importance, and yet we must keep working, caring for children, spouses, and partners and all of their activities and needs. In between doctor's appointments, meetings with hospice workers, basketball games, graduations, board meetings, and work deadlines, it is easy to lose our balance.

When we love and care for someone who is dying, a few things are important to do—no matter what. First and foremost, we have to hang on to our health and sanity. We will be of no use to anyone if we are exhausted, sick, and at our wit's end. It is time to call in the troops: professional services, family members, and friends. If it "takes a village to raise a child," it also takes a village to help a loved one pass on in comfort and dignity. We have to eat well, sleep enough, and get out into the sunshine and fresh air. These things are not optional. We have to manage our stress in whatever ways work for us: yoga in the morning, a walk after work, reading a good book, having coffee with a friend, or extra visits to our therapist. Short-term stress is hard on our bodies, but the effect of accumulated, long-term stress can be devastating to us physically, mentally, and emotionally. Whatever it takes—we must, must, must make time to care for ourselves.

An important quality we need to cultivate in this time is acceptance—not just accepting that someone we love is dying, but acceptance of them, ourselves, and other family members. This acceptance can be tough to achieve. Our loved one is not going to become another person just because they are dying. They might soften, open up, or reach out in new ways, but the person they are will only grow in clarity and strength. All that is superfluous will fall away. We might be surprised by rarely seen qualities, but they have always been there.

This is as true for us as it is for the loved one who is dying. Many qualities and skills are needed in a family or circle of friends caring for a dying person. We might not be good at emptying bedpans, but if we are good at fixing things or managing money, we will find things that need fixing or money that will need managing. On the other hand, if we are people who need to be doing something, *anything,* in a crisis, we might be happier emptying bedpans than doing nothing at all. If we have a gift for honest conversation with young people, we could be a priceless piece of the experience for them as they struggle with their fears and confusion. Each of us will feel pulled to expressions of love, concern, and contribution from the deep places in ourselves. Laughter can be wonderful; so can music and prayers. Instead, we bring the qualities of who we are—the best qualities—and find where they are needed in different roles.

> *My relationship with my parents was tender, loving, and supportive no matter what. I think of my dad's strong hands beside me as a child . . . and I think of my hands on his cheek as I shaved him before he died. I think of my mom's hands mixing the biscuit bread as I looked over the edge of the table as a child, waiting with anticipation . . . and I think of my arms holding her as she died, her beautiful long black hair spread on the pillow. Such tenderness in the circle of life with them . . . and how lucky I am.*
>
> ~ Merita T., 62-year-old

We must be honest with ourselves and our families. This is not about feeling guilty if we cannot visit every day or stay up all night at the hospital. We need to let masks drop away and say what we can handle. If we are the sibling who likes to make a joke to keep things from getting too heavy, we can own that sensitivity with our sisters and brothers by explaining that it helps us manage our feelings. If we are a person who needs a good cry periodically to clear away stress, then we can sit down with someone who will let us do that and let 'er rip! If it all feels like too much, or we cannot be hands-on with a loved one who is dying, we need to express that and find other ways to be in touch and provide support: cards, calls, encouragement, money, and providing respite. That support and love is vital, not only to the dying person, but also to the family or friends who are caretakers.

> *I never spent much time with my family after I was grown, but in my forties, both of my parents got sick, and suddenly I wanted to be there. I moved back and took on my part, fully and completely, with my heart wide open—no reservations and no holding back. It was where I wanted to be. My family needed me and I was ready.*
>
> ~ 47-year-old

We need to honor this process in ourselves, our family members, and friends. We will step up at our own pace, opening our hearts to new levels of love and feelings, and that happens for each of us in different ways and at different times. Some of us who thought we could be there might realize that it is more than we can handle. This can be hard to accept in ourselves and our loved ones, and can lead to families being torn apart by the stress. We cannot make ourselves or anyone else be someplace we are not ready to be. We might show up out of duty or guilt, but our hearts will not be there until we are ready. As we can, we open our arms and provide the opportunity to welcome each other into new relationships, openheartedness, and acceptance. Not everybody will take the opportunity, but many family members will, and we will find ourselves in a closer, richer, more loving family for doing it.

The circle of people surrounding a dying person is not a static thing, because life continues for us with all of its complications. It is more of a dance: we take turns, rest, stand strong, and pull away. In that fluid movement, the circle stays steady, but each one of us can take the time and space to stay healthy and balanced.

> *When my mom was dying, my sisters and I had to figure out a lot of stuff. I'm the oldest, and in the beginning, there were things we all had assumptions about. But sometimes I couldn't manage anything, and they stepped up and took care of things. I had to let go of being "big sister" and they had to let go of being "little sisters." We were all grown women, and we needed to work together. Our motto was, "Just tell the truth about how you feel and what you need, and we'll work it out." It changed our relationships— deepened and enriched them. What we learned during that sad time has been nothing but a gift ever since.*
>
> ~ 46-year-old

The Emotional Process

The last, best gift we can give somebody we love is to help them live as long and as well as they can and then help them die the way they wish. For almost everyone, the basic wishes are simple: we want to die peacefully, gently, with love, comfort, and dignity, surrounded by our loved ones. That is not always the way it happens. The passing of a loved one can be a long and strenuous process, and all of us will doubt our strength sometimes. So much is changing and so much is needed. We may react first to physical changes and problems. If our loved one used to be strong and fit, and now we see them shrinking or wasting away, we will definitely have a reaction to the change. We will also react to mental and emotional changes. Elizabeth Kübler-Ross's five stages of grief include the understanding that the common responses of anger, denial, bargaining, depression, and acceptance are not absolutes. They can occur in any order or not at all, and they often begin before the loss occurs. Unless a loved one dies suddenly, many of us will grieve the changes and losses every step of the way, even while our loved one is still alive.

A parent's dying is particularly complicated because the very fabric of the family as we have known it is changing. Nothing is the way it used to be, which can be frightening as we begin to worry about what life will be like without them. For instance, if Mom has always been communication central for a far-flung family, how will we communicate when she is gone? If our parents' home used to be the holiday gathering place, who will host now? Are we even going to gather anymore? Our contradictory feelings can be confusing.

In the last few weeks of my mother's life, I suddenly realized that I didn't know how to make some of my favorite meals that she used to cook. Here she was dying, and the big thing I wanted to ask her about was recipes! I felt so torn and confused, even guilty. I didn't want to bother her with such silly stuff, but it felt very important to me. I kept thinking, "Why did I wait so long? Why didn't I ask her before?"

~ 48-year-old

Every family member and friend goes through a huge emotional/psychological process. Those who live far away will struggle with feelings different from those who carry the responsibilities of day-to-day care. Each time we visit, we have to confront the growing losses anew. We can experience profound shock when we visit again, even if we have been gone only a few weeks or months. The terrible fear and grief are almost overwhelming when it is time to leave. Will we ever see them again? Is this the last time?

If we are part of the caretaking on a regular basis, we often cannot clearly see the gradual changes in our loved one. Instead we are caught in the confusing push and pull of love and exhaustion.

We might feel guilty to admit that because we are so tired, and their suffering seems to have no end, we want them to go. When a young person is dying, we may fight endlessly to keep them here—even though they are suffering—because dying so young is not right. Despite the fact that our feelings are completely normal, we are shocked when they surface. It takes time to accept the emotional contradictions of loving someone who is dying.

> *Both of my parents are on in-home hospice care. My Papa, who is bedridden and has trouble seeing clearly, often lies in his bed surrounded by sounds and people who don't talk much to him, only care for his physical needs. Since I live out of town, I try to spend a lot of time sitting with him when I visit. Late one night, when everything was quiet, I saw he was awake. I pulled up a chair next to him and started asking him questions about his life. For three and a half hours, he regaled me with stories of his childhood, the war, my Momma, and his children. It was three and a half hours I will never forget. I was truly blessed with that extraordinary time with him. Now I do it every time I go back and most recently recorded his voice so that I would always have him with me.*
>
> ~ Nancy G., 56-year-old

The dying person is often way ahead of us in the process of letting go. They may become powerful teachers as we learn to stay with the love and release everything else. This is the gift that many of us have learned from dying loved ones, the secret that allows us to be with them in the fullest way possible: stay with the love and let go of the past and the old ways of doing things. Every moment that we put aside busyness and expectations is a moment we can be present with them, without distractions and fears pulling us away.

We can feel healing and peace in those quiet places, where memories are gifts of love, and tears and words are gifts of gratitude. For most of us, including the dying person, that space will come and go. Sometimes we will be very connected, and other times we will just want to wail or fight or make a big scene. Our understanding and acceptance of the ebb and flow will help to soften the process. We all do the best we can.

> *"Just sit with me for a little while," my friend Opalanga would sometimes ask when I arrived for my evening shift as a caretaker. I would have just come from a day at work and then traveled through rush hour traffic to get there. In that frame of mind, I'd be checking the medicine list, getting updates from the afternoon caretaker, looking at the food planned for dinner, and checking phone messages. Her soft voice would stop me in my tracks, and then I'd remember to sit down and let myself enter the gentle, loving space of her home and her presence.*
>
> ~ Jane T., 56-year-old

Not everyone will make their transition pain-free, in peace, and surrounded by loved ones. That is a real gift, but for many individuals and families, the ending is not so gentle. Our loved one might die unexpectedly from an accident or sudden health condition. Of course that can happen at any time, and is, for most who have faced it, the most stunning experience of our lives. Survivors, with no control or choice, are left in a nightmare of shock, disbelief, and regrets. Those of us who have gone through this experience know how much time and love it takes to find balance and peace again.

For others, the long road of good-bye is filled with pain and suffering, or chaos and anger. When someone we love is suffering the raging pain of sickle cell anemia or the drowning confusion of dementia, we will suffer too.

The best I can explain what it is like living with someone who has Alzheimer's is you no longer live in your world... you live in theirs.

~ Sally D., 44-year-old

For almost three and a half decades, my beloved husband, Larry, and I have shared lives, experiences, tragedies, joys, laughter, dancing, stories, and songs together. Now, as he has had Alzheimer's for over five years, we cherish the good times and remember to remember that it is the laughter, dancing, singing, and stories that have kept us loving each other for all this time. I berate myself for not knowing at any given time whether he is cognizant or fuzzy, out of it or right on target. I find myself expecting too much and not being nearly patient enough. I try to forgive myself, knowing that he may not remember, but I remember, and this greatly saddens me. He is mostly fine in the present moment, yet more and more our shared memory, the intimate and endearing images, experiences, and journeys of us are being lost. Since most of my blood family has dismissed us, some of the memory of my and our life story is slipping away. Such deep loss. Yet our family of heart is with us in all ways, supportive and with listening hearts. I revel in small successes, and I get help with cleaning. I also get massages and Reiki. I love being with cherished friends and family of heart, but I often feel that I just grab time. And sometimes Larry will come clear with wonder, a bright clarity of image or emotion that is amazingly endearing. So I bless these moments, hug him all the more, and dance in his arms again.

~ Cherie S., 62-year-old

We will need all of our resources—family and friends, spiritual community, healthcare providers, and all of our support groups and systems—to assist us. Watching a loved one suffer and not being able to help feels like a nightmare. If we have been through this experience, we might admit that the first, most profound feeling at the passing of our loved one was relief—for them and for ourselves.

> *My mother's death affected me the most. Initially because she talked on the phone to me twice a week and asked me how I was feeling and what I was thinking. My mother's absence from my life was massive. My image was of the negative space experienced with a tidal wave and then the influx of power and pain as the space fills up. All the gifts of my mother's love, care, attention and life presence became painfully conscious with her absence.*
>
> ~ Carol Sch., 64-year-old

What if the struggles are emotional? What if a dying parent was abusive? Or absent? What if it is an ex-spouse or partner who cheated on us? What if our loved one committed suicide? Here in Middlehood, we know that human relationships are complicated, and few of us have found our way to this point without encountering at least one relationship that was tangled, painful, or harmful. In the past, we may have taxed the listening power of our friends and family while we let go and moved on from a difficult relationship. We may even have needed to spend time in therapy or recovery groups, trying to find our way to a place of peace. But hopefully we have done the work and are in a clear place about those relationships, because nothing has the power to throw us into chaos like the death of someone with whom we have painful or unresolved issues.

If we have already made the puma choice, we will be well into the work of resolution with ourselves and our relationships by this time in our lives. If we have not, it is vital that we get started. The wisdom of the Equation for Transformation may or may not benefit the person who is dying, but it will surely benefit us. Doing this work will not prevent all the varied emotions of loss, but it can help us unclutter the process of saying good-bye and leave us clearer and healthier after the person is gone.

Grief in Middlehood

Here in Middlehood, we are not less affected by loss than we used to be, but we may be more experienced at dealing with our grief. We are also not alone in our sadness as we might have been when we were young. Now we are surrounded by people who understand what it feels like to lose a loved one, so they are not afraid of our sadness. They stay close and remind us of elemental things: to eat well, sleep, and rest as best we can. They help us remember how to find feelings of peace by putting ourselves in the bigger picture of life: watching the sun rise and set, looking at stars, listening to music, and being with people we love.

> *I've always found that any significant experience that brings intense joy or pain can alter perceptions, feelings, and actions. For example, the death of my sister and mother has made me cherish others in my life and has changed what's important in my life (people over things).*
>
> ~ Teri B., 53-year-old

We are also wiser about what constitutes our grief than we used to be. Now our sadness has two visible parts: the loss of the person we love and all that they meant to us; and the loss of a piece of ourselves that was tied to that person: the hopes, dreams, security, or personal history. Our experiences tell us that the only true healing after losing someone we love is time, and we have to let time do its work. We may be impatient with the pace, but "take a step and breathe," our mantra of life and growth, will sooner or later lead us back to our lives and the people and things we love.

After my husband, Ned, died, it took me two years to regain any normalcy in my life. I thought that I would jump right back into exercise, but I didn't. I thought that I would go on a diet, but I didn't. I spent most of the first year after his death going through photographs. The photos of our wonderful life together were my solace. I found my support group in a neighbor and friend who had lost her husband three months before my husband's death. We had all known each other, so that made our relationship even more meaningful. But most important of all was that commonality of being able to speak freely about our deceased husbands. At first, that was the only topic of conversation, but with the passage of time, the need to speak about them and hear their names spoken slowly receded. As time went on, I started making new friends, developing new hobbies, traveling, volunteering, and exercising. Ned always lived life to its fullest, and I know that he would be disappointed if I were to live it any less so. Life is short, and we have been blessed to be able to experience it, so I say get out there and make the most of it!

~ Sally V., 65-year-old

The other part of our grief, the loss of a piece of ourselves, is where we can be more active. Over and over throughout our lives, we have given away pieces of ourselves—to other people, beliefs, causes, or work. And over and over we have learned to take back what we gave away and keep ourselves whole. This is as true following the death of a loved one as it is following a divorce or the loss of a job. No matter how much we loved the other person, no matter how much we shared, we are whole beings, and the history, dreams, and hopes are ours, with them or without them. We may change some of the dreams or modify some hopes, but laying claim to them again or finding new ways to express them will help us heal.

> *Being strong to me means holding those in pain till they can release the burden, or at least know some comfort from what they were challenged to endure and what it means to come out to the other side of those life-changing challenges. Giving when you think you can't and then remembering to replenish so you can continue to help yourself and others.*
>
> ~ Terry L., 56-year-old

For most young people, losing a loved one is an isolated experience, and not until Middlehood do we see how our losses string together, creating a kind of accumulated grief. It is as though everyone we love is tied on one thread wrapped around our hearts. Each time we lose someone, we feel the sadness of the other losses.

> *As soon as my father got home from my mother's memorial service, he sat down on a step, put his head in his hands, and cried, "First my mother dies and now my wife dies." My siblings and I had no idea how to respond. His mother had died when he was a little boy—more than sixty years before! Now, years later, I understand. In that moment, there was no time; there was only his devastating loss of the two most important women in his life.*
>
> ~ 53-year-old

When our parents and elders die at the end of a long and reasonably happy life, we miss them terribly, but we can accept that sadness. If we are mature adults when this passing happens, our lives have probably given us the skills we need to handle it. And even more, all of life rallies to support the living when the elders pass on. Our relatives, children, friends, parents' friends, everybody will be present to help the generational shift happen because it is the natural order—the way it is supposed to be. Even if we have not lost our parents yet, we recognize what is going on. This is how one generation teaches the next and prepares them for their turn. It is as much an image of family as a young couple with a new baby. As the older generation fades, the Middlehood generation rises, and the young begin their training.

But our feelings are different when a young parent or spouse/partner dies in the prime of life.

I met Cynthia after her divorce from her husband and as she picked up the pieces with her three young sons. I was part of her healing process, and both of us had felt like we were drowning in our previous relationships. In our process of healing, a tiny crack opened in the door of fate, and we both took full advantage and seized the day . . . carpe diem . . . no turning back. Wow, was it worth it! In the short time, only five years we spent together, we became soul mates and experienced unconditional love and happiness. She died of cancer, and although she is no longer physically with me, the memories will carry me throughout my lifetime and bring me comfort until we meet again.

~ Monique M., 54-year-old

Our feelings are especially difficult when death happens out of its natural order, such as when a child or young person dies. Then everybody is lost. On every level—in our cells, in our bones and heart, everywhere—every bit of us screams, "This is wrong, wrong, wrong! This is not how it is supposed to be!" Nobody knows what to say. Family and friends are often at a loss for how to help; they cannot even imagine the loss if they have not been through it. The death of a child or young person leaves a hole that never fills in. Parents and family members who have lost a young person never get over the loss, but with time and love and healing, we will carry the loss and let go of the feeling that our lives have ended. Our lives have not ended, no matter how much pain and grief we carry. Our lives may feel smaller because more space is given to what has been lost, but staggering, limping, or even crawling, we are still here. A great deal of time and the love of people who understand can help us—not to forget but to stretch our hearts to love the one who is gone and to love the ones who are still here.

My Sister, Linda Sue by Nancy Geha

I was only twenty years old when my sister Linda died. She was a year older—smart, kind, beautiful, and sensitive. Even though we came from a large family of twelve children, she and I were very close, not only sisters, but best friends. When Linda was sixteen years old, she contracted hepatitis B from a blood transfusion. For the next five years, she struggled and suffered from the disease, the treatments, and her numerous physicians' lack of knowledge and resources. At the age of twenty-one, my sweet sister died from complications of liver failure. My family was devastated. We had lost a precious young woman who had really wanted to live. My Momma took to her bed for weeks. Papa continued to work at his furniture business in spite of his incredible grief because, no matter how he felt, he needed to take care of his family. Most of us suffered silently, grieving in our own private ways. No one really spoke about Linda. The younger children didn't understand why their sister was no longer there. The older ones stayed quiet so they could help take care of the little ones, to keep going in the face of their extraordinary sadness.

My family's lives were turned upside down. It was the first time we had faced the death of a loved one, especially one as young and close as my sister. I myself denied her health was failing most of the time she was sick. I just knew she would be cured. After all, she was only twenty-one! She seemed to know, though, that she would not be with us much longer. When she would try to tell me how she felt, I dismissed it. I couldn't possibly think about the unthinkable. The night she went into a coma, I was with her. To this day, I still wish I had said so many things to her before she died and listened to her feelings along the way. As the years have gone by, my pain has lessened, but my sadness continues, and I know in my heart that she did know that I loved her with all my heart.

Thirty-nine years later I still miss her and wish she was here for me to share our lives. But I will always be grateful for the twenty-one years we were blessed with her presence, love, and insight. I will always feel honored to have known and loved her as my sister and my best friend.

Becoming the Older Generation

"Take a step and breathe, take a step and breathe . . ." Up the mountain we go. Our grandparents and older relatives are probably gone now, and our parents are leaving. *We* are becoming the older generation. Most of us are staggered by the prospect. We are not ready! How can it be time for that? We do not know enough yet! Aren't we still young? It seems like only yesterday we were fighting with our parents about the length of our skirts or how to potty train our first child. We have been grown-ups for a long time now, but the difference between being grown and being the older generation is enormous.

Whether or not we are ready, the great shift is upon us—the end of an era has come. The passing of our parents and other elders is an enormous change. We miss them as individuals, the sound of their voices, and the feel of their hugs, but we also miss them as a generation. We miss feeling there is someone who knows better than we do, someone who can be relied on when we are overwhelmed or stuck. We mourn the loss of all the memories, history, stories, knowledge, and perspective that they held. As an African proverb says, "When an elder dies, it is as if a library has burned."

Being an only child has its ups and downs. The upside is that I have no siblings to fight with. The downside is that I have no one to help share the responsibilities when one loses a parent. As a child, you never think about losing a parent. You see them as invincible and think they will live forever. When I took my dad to the hospital to find out that he had cancer, I was daddy's little girl who had to become an adult. I went from my dad taking care of me to me taking care of my dad. My mom and I made sure we granted him his last wish to be as comfortable as possible at home until he passed on. Adjusting to life without my dad has been tough but manageable. I work a full-time job and take care of my mom on the weekends. She is still somewhat independent but doesn't drive so I have to make sure she gets her errands done when we are together. My dad took care of everything, and it has become so clear how much he did for us. Even though it felt like my life stopped when he died, the world kept on going. It is something I have had to learn to accept. There are days where I seem to keep it together, and there are days I will burst into tears without any notice. I'll run across e-mails he sent or other precious things, and they bring me to tears. It's those little things I have to live without and it's painful. I know it's okay to cry. No one should ever tell you that you can't cry for the ones you love. My dad has been gone for almost two years, but it still feels like yesterday. There is no timeline for grief, and I am learning that the pain will subside in time, but the sadness will last always. I know it will be okay and I know that I will be okay.

~ Lisa M., 42-year-old

We feel hesitant and inadequate as we step up to the role of being the older generation. No doubt our parents felt the same when it was their turn, and our children will certainly know the same sense of inadequacy when we pass the wand to them.

We've been talking with our cousins, because if we want to have any kind of family, it can't be through the old people anymore. When I first realized that—it felt kind of sad— like, who do we look to? I'm not ready to be the elder! I always enjoyed the older people and could listen to their stories forever. Now, what am I gonna say to these young people? I haven't even figured what I don't know yet, and now there isn't anyone there to ask! It's like we're the keepers of family history all of a sudden . . . and we don't have a lot of it. How inadequate we are! How diluted it gets!

~ Jan S., 55-year-old

No matter how old we are or our parents are, they know us— not just remember us—as the children and young people we were. As our parents pass on, they take that knowing with them. Even though our siblings remember some things, and photos and family stories help, there is no one left to miss us as the kids we once were. Suddenly, part of our life, our past, is receding. Clear chapters exist in our lives in a way they did not before. And strangely, despite partners/spouses, children, grandchildren, siblings, relatives, and friends, we occasionally feel lonely for someone or something we cannot quite name.

To further complicate things, we are not elders yet, despite the opinions of children who think we are old. Our relatives and friends in their eighties often remind us of that when they say longingly, "Oh, to be sixty again!" We are in the process of becoming elders, but right now we are moving through the middle—looking back on more than half a lifetime and looking ahead at the years to come. We are watching young people and wondering how we can help them learn what they need to learn, and at the same time, we are watching our guides and role models show us what to do and what not to do as we get older.

We cannot afford to take life for granted anymore. With each good-bye we say to a loved one passing on, we know more clearly that someday, the good-bye will be ours. No matter how many years we have left to live, we could die tomorrow. That knowledge is one of the greatest fears and greatest gifts of Middlehood. With each loss, the impetus to make every day count and not waste time on silly, insignificant things becomes more powerful. We learn to stay with the love and let go of everything else. We put our attention on what is life-giving and valuable. We learn to carry our sadness and sorrows with us. We miss our beloved ones who have made their transition, but we know that life keeps going... and so do we.

This is the beginning of real wisdom, and it will continue to grow with us for the rest of our lives. Take a step and breathe... this is the way of the puma.

Reflection Questions

- Have I made the puma choice for myself? If I have, how have my feelings and thoughts about death and life changed? If I have not, what is my next step towards an acceptance of death?
- How have I been changed by the death of a loved one? How have my experience(s) with death challenged my beliefs or deepened them?

- If someone I love is dying, how can I help them through the end of their life? What can I do for myself to help me through the process?
- How do I deal with grief? What kind of support do I have?

CHAPTER 10

Work: Ready to Retire or Just Getting Started?

The happiest people I've ever met, regardless of their profession, their social standing, or their economic status, are people that are fully engaged in the world around them. The most fulfilled people are the ones who get up every morning and stand for something larger than themselves. They are the people who care about others, who will extend a helping hand to someone in need or will speak up about an injustice when they see it.

> ~ Wilma Mankiller, *Northeastern State University, Tahlequah, OK, 2009 commencement address*

You must listen, hard and deep, to that which inspires you. To the task you were put on this earth to complete. And follow that voice.

> ~ Judy Baca, *UCLA School of Art and Architecture, 2012 commencement address*

BUSY, BUSY, BUSY! ASK NEARLY ANY Middlehood woman how she is, and that will likely be her answer. We are juggling our children and grandchildren, aging parents, spouses/partners, jobs, projects, and friends. We could be raising money for a foundation or raising kids, or both. We could be sitting in a board meeting or by the bedside of an elderly parent, or both. The point is—we are Middlehood women, and everything is both possible and even likely to be going on during this phase of our lives. We have always struggled to balance our various loves and commitments, but right now, there is definitely not enough of us to go around.

> *My poor dad. . . . He really wanted me to come and visit more often, and stay longer when I came. I knew he was lonely after my mom died, so I came as much as I could. One time when he was sad that I was leaving, he said irritably, "Well, just tell that boss of yours that you need more time off!" I had to laugh when I said, "Dad, that's the problem. I can't take more time off because I'm the boss!"*
>
> ~ 55-year-old

Work is a big question these days. We could be at the top of our game in our careers, working long hours, and maybe even making lots of money. We could be filled with the excitement and anxiety of starting back to work after years as a stay- at-home mom. We could be passionately rearranging everything in order to launch a new career or start a new business. Or we could be tired of it all and spend our days longing for retirement after decades of work. All of these are possible scenarios for working Middlehood women. But just as in other areas of our lives, we are in transition. Even though our feelings about work in our early forties are distinctly different from our feelings about work in our early sixties, this is when the changes begin.

Our futures are no longer a series of unending "somedays," and our priorities are beginning to change. How do we choose those priorities? Each of us will have a different way of deciding, based on our experiences and the choices we have made in the past. The common factor, the thread that begins now, is the work of preparing for our elder years. We are not elders yet, but the reason we have begun to identify more with our elders is that they hold the key to helping us determine what is most important as we adjust our focus. We might hesitate to ask, "I am getting old, so what do I need to do?" But the pressure to prepare has begun. It is imperative to make plans and decisions for the future. For instance, we have to take our finances, as well as our health and healthcare, seriously. We cannot just "see what happens" anymore.

My soon to be ex-husband decided he didn't want to be married anymore, and my vision of retirement took an abrupt turn. That combined with my father being ill has challenged me. I am struggling with the stigma of being twice divorced and having to face retirement alone. On the other hand—now I can do whatever I want, and no one is trying to influence my decisions. I think that initial fear of doing things alone was my concern.

~ Deb McB., 50-year-old

Middlehood can be a prime time to lose track of ourselves if we do not begin preparing for our futures. Despite busy lives, we need to think about what we want for the rest of our lives. We may find ourselves making new lists or asking different questions about things we have not done or completed yet. Whatever these lists and questions look like, we must make time to consider them so that we do not get ambushed by our overworked minds and bodies.

One of the questions that is guaranteed to surface is, "How am I feeling about my life right now?" That one question opens up an avalanche of responses. We could love and feel satisfied by our work, relationships, and lives. We could be bored or frustrated with our jobs, overwhelmed with family needs, struggling with financial problems, or lonely in a long-term relationship. We might have just lost someone close or had a serious health issue of our own, and feel sad or anxious about the future. Exciting new possibilities on the horizon might fill us with excitement and hope. Turbulent feelings of transition and change could be keeping us awake at night. Most likely, the list of feelings is a long one because we are feeling ten or twelve of them at once!

Another set of questions could begin with, "What am I doing?" We could ask that in a couple of different ways. For instance, "*What* am I doing? and "What am I *doing*?" might net us different answers and feelings. The really loaded question is, "What do I *want* to do?" Part of the restlessness of Middlehood comes directly from facing that question and listening to our varied answers. Are we still happy with our old jobs and activities, or do we long for something new, something deeper, something more challenging?

> *The world is not organized to appreciate my gifts. I'm not an entrepreneur, ambitious for money, nor independently wealthy, but the work I like to do does not pay . . . life is passing me by so quickly that certain options are closing. I don't want to go back to school for another degree because of time and money. I don't know how to fit into some of the cultural changes or how to survive them.*
>
> ~ Rhea M., 58-year-old

> *I loved staying at home with my kids when they were young, but they're big now, and I'm excited about going back to work. I know a lot has changed in the last fifteen years, but I'm looking forward to learning new things.*
>
> ~ 42-year-old

It wasn't always true, but these days each generation seems to grow up with vastly different goals and expectations about adult life and work. For instance, there was a huge difference between the baby boomers and their parents. The generation born in the 1920s and 1930s grew up during the Depression or soon after. Everything about planning for the future had to do with taking care of family. The Depression and its legacy taught them to plan their lives in great detail and save money for the future. Security was the most important thing, and the only success they could count on came by their own hard work and sacrifice.

The next generation was born after World War II, when young soldiers came home, and prosperity began to grow. But it was also after the atom bomb was dropped in Japan, and early baby boomers grew up with a strange combination of hope and fear: hope because the economy was growing and life seemed to be improving, and fear that the world could be wiped out in a few minutes. Perhaps one of the slogans from the 1960s makes sense given the strange times: Live for today! Life was good but maybe short, so living and loving in the moment was important.

Of course all baby boomers did not grow up with only a "live for today" mentality, but we also did not plan for every penny and every minute of our lives as our parents did. We watched social justice and peace movements bring about huge changes in the world and assumed that change and growth were possible, even inevitable. Probably our most pervasive belief was that we had the right to fulfill ourselves and our potential. For many of us, work was not just about skills or a way to get money to support our family. Work became an act of love and service or self-expression, not just a job. Our parents may have felt real pride about their work, loved and valued what they were doing, but most of them did not talk about their work as fulfilling or as part of changing the world. This shift in attitude about work has had a profound effect on boomers, their children, and everyone who has come after.

I've been lucky to have had enough success to help me be relaxed about "accomplishing" more at this stage of my

life. I've been blessed with so many rich and interesting
relationships.

~ Barbara B., 59-year-old

Work, Job and Career

Because the meaning and purpose of work is no longer as
simple as it used to be, we must have a way to talk about work
that incorporates those changes. The definition of *work* is varied
and complex, but a theme recurs: the use of energy and effort to
accomplish something. According to *Merriam-Webster's Collegiate
Dictionary (11th edition)*, *work* is "activity in which one exerts
strength or faculties to do or perform something: . . . to overcome
obstacles and achieve an objective or result"; or it's "something
produced or accomplished by effort, exertion, or exercise of skill . . .
or creative talent." At its core, the word *work* could be "one's
accustomed means of livelihood," but it also may have nothing to
do with getting paid or earning a salary and health benefits.

> *I think, at this time in my life, that professional options*
> *are more numerous, because I'm less bound by others'*
> *expectations and beliefs about what I should do or am able*
> *to do. I can still do or start anything! I do think there is*
> *considerable age discrimination out there, but I am not*
> *as afraid of it holding me back as I might be if I wanted*
> *traditional work.*

~ Wendy C., 54-year-old

What makes a job different from work? Again, according to
Merriam-Webster, a *job* is a "piece of work"; "something that has to
be done: task"; or it's a "specific duty, role, or function." And a *career*
is a "field for or pursuit of consecutive progressive achievement"

or a "profession for which one trains and which is undertaken as a permanent calling."

To simplify this discussion, let us differentiate between our jobs and our work by incorporating a couple of definitions. Let us say that work is actually our Work (with a capital *W*): our calling that we accomplish through creative talent, skill, and effort. Our jobs could be a piece of our Work, or they could simply be a task or specific role we undertake to make a living. And for this discussion, let us assume that a career could be either a calling or a long-term job(s) that we have trained for and through which we have accomplished various goals over time.

What stands out from these simplified concepts is that our Work, job, and career can be the same, but they also may differ greatly. For instance, if we raised children, we know that is some of the most significant Work we have ever done in our lives, and we never made any money doing it. How about those of us who have retail jobs during the day and then write, paint, or play music at night? Isn't one our job and the other our Work? If we had a calling to teach science or history but became disillusioned or burned out because of circumstances or politics, is it still our career even if it no longer feels like our Work? Has it become just a job?

If we found our Work early on, we know the feeling of fitting into what we are doing. There is a rightness to it, and we have deep reserves of energy, creativity, and excitement no matter how taxing or challenging it is. But some of us are late bloomers and did not find our Work as young people. Is it still whispering quietly to us? Do we even know what our Work is? What if we have a calling or talent for more than one thing? It can be really complicated.

There are many more variations of our work lives than these three, but they are good concepts to explore as we feel the pull to Middlehood sorting. Why be so picky about defining them? For two reasons: a) we have spent an enormous part of the last twenty or thirty years doing what we do to make a living and/or raise our children; and b) it makes a big difference when we think and plan for our futures.

For many women, a subtle but powerful development begins in our late thirties and early forties: the growing awareness that we are finally "old enough" and that we really *know* something. We want to be taken seriously, and we want our job experience, life experience, and knowledge to count for something. We are not the up-and-coming, full-of-potential young people anymore. Now we are the experienced ones, becoming authorities and experts, mentors and teachers. It feels good being the expert rather than the beginner. We want a better salary, more authority and leadership opportunities, the chance and resources to be more creative, and ways to apply everything we have learned through decades of life and experience.

At this point we feel the enormous differences between those of us in early Middlehood and those of us in later Middlehood.

I am in the middle, age-wise, in my school, and I sometimes feel lonely because it can be difficult to connect with other teachers. A majority of them are in their early thirties or younger. They talk about going out dancing or to a bar, the guys they are dating or are engaged to marry. I sometimes feel like I'm one of them, and I want to be, but I don't really have a lot in common with them. My interests and energy levels are a lot different from theirs. I feel more in sync with the older teachers, but I don't always connect with them either, because the way they approach teaching is different than the way I do. Also, they are anxious to finish their careers in the most positive way they can, and I still have a lot of years to go, even though I'm going to be one of them in the not-too-distant future.

~ Paige T., 45-year-old

In our early to midforties, we expect to work for at least two more decades, and our accomplishments, status, and salaries are important. It is here that we begin to feel restless if we are not in a job or position that suits us. We are ready to flex our muscles, and if our job situations are too small or boring, we are not happy. We have many skills; we want them to matter and to be recognized. After work, we have rich lives full of family and children, friends and recreation that are consciously chosen. Our time is precious, and we opt for spending both work and recreational time on activities we really value. We may find ourselves looking for a new job because we have outgrown our old one or need to move on to someplace that will appreciate us.

Many of us share these feelings to some extent, but the situation is more complex for single women. If we are the only one paying the bills and saving for retirement, the pressure to find and keep a well-paying job is enormous and is doubly true for single moms. If we are not part of a team working to take care of ourselves and our children, we do not have a safety net. We still have the need for respect and appreciation but might not feel able to risk a secure position to take a step towards fulfilling a dream.

These needs grow stronger and stronger through our forties and into our fifties, and then—something else begins to happen. Just at the point when we feel that we have become expert in our field and have great confidence in our abilities and knowledge, the pendulum shifts. Suddenly, we have the sneaking feeling that we may not count as much anymore. All our lives we were told that increasing our experience was vital for our careers. Now it seems that experience is only important to younger people who are just building careers. We have experience, insights, the ability to see patterns over time, and skills we have honed to a sharp edge, but that does not seem to matter much anymore. Our bosses are getting younger, the technology is getting more complicated, and we may find ourselves growing angry or unhappy because we do not feel respected, and our experience is becoming irrelevant. We can feel confused, even a little scared, to know that our younger bosses, who have decision-making power over us, may not understand the skills and experience we have to offer.

It is not this way in all cultures, but in many, we miss out on the natural aging into wisdom and elderhood transition. We learned to expect *this* progression: 1) we learn and work and establish a body of knowledge; 2) we use our experience and become an authority in that area; and 3) we grow into a wise and respected elder, with young people eager to absorb some of our knowledge. But not many of us reach this ideal. Instead, just as we are hitting our peak, the culmination of decades of knowledge and experience, we are tossed on the downward slide because we are getting too old. And we may cost too much—so in a bad economy, we are usually the ones who are let go.

> *I think one of the results of being laid off was losing a good deal of my self-confidence—sense of worth and ability to do a job well . . . with bouts of doubts and self-pity thrown in some days! It came as a blow—a surprise and a "heck, what am I going to do now?" feeling. I think it's especially true for those of us who have been with a company for a long time, especially one that we believe in. It triggered a chronic self-esteem issue of mine, where it's hard to believe in myself even when others believe in me. I wasn't the only person to be laid off and that helped a little. We were provided out-placement services, which were not very helpful, but I met some good people and found support from fellow job seekers. If there was a good part to all of it, at least I was often able to structure my day as I wanted: job search, job search, job search, exercise class. If I had a way to support myself and not work, I would grab it—it was very nice to make my own schedule. But I do like a paycheck! So growth, new skills, and new friends, a calmer here and now approach to the day, a clearer*

understanding of integrity, and a renewed confidence are some of the outcomes of being unemployed and the search for a new job. I did find a new job at last, and now I do my best to be a wonderful bank teller. I've always wanted to be a bank teller—for a while at least—now until I retire?

~ Susan F., 60-year-old

Susan's story is a perfect example of the tumult of feelings we will need to sort out if we lose our place in the work world against our will. Above all, it feels incredibly unfair. But sort we must, or we will find ourselves stuck in a loop of paralyzing hopelessness and fear. Susan's natural ability to work the process of the Equation for Transformation is a powerful example of how we can turn challenging situations into possibilities for growth and expansion. First, she grappled with her feelings, her resistance to the forced change, and the grief of letting go of a job she loved. As she shifted into the middle stage, she recognized the positive pieces around her and allowed a kind of active waiting to happen. Finally, as a new door opened, she was ready and able to walk through it with hope and gratitude. Not everyone's story will have such a happy ending, but Susan's flexibility and focus on the bigger picture of her life gave her the ability to turn a disaster into a new chapter.

This is a strange time for those of us in our fifties and early sixties. On the one hand, we are confident, knowledgeable, and well settled into our careers and work lives. We know what we are good at and we know what we need. We are far less likely to search for a new job every couple of years, much more content to stay in a good job. If we love our work, we may be happy to keep working for quite a while yet.

And most of us are delighted to work with younger people who have new ideas and a fresh take on things. We have worked long enough to understand that a vital, creative workplace always includes a variety of people, talents, and ideas. Inexperienced workers entering the workplace bring new research, enthusiasm, skills, and perspective. What they do not have yet is the instinct or intuition that comes with experience, one of the indefinable, hard to explain aspects of our work when we reach our forties and fifties.

It's a bit like driving. A good young driver will absolutely have faster reflexes and better eyesight than a good Middlehood driver. But how can those of us who have driven for decades explain the experience and instinct, or "knowing," that help us predict what other drivers are going to do?

> *I just knew that little boy was going to run out in front of my car. I don't know how I knew it, but I saw him on the grass playing, and the next thing I knew, he ran right into me from between two parked cars. Thank heaven I had already started to slow down, or I would have hit him instead of him running into me. It was a terrifying near miss, and I'm so glad I paid attention to my intuition!*
>
> ~ 44-year-old

Many of us have stories like these: that gut feeling that a car is going to pull out in front of us or try to pass when there is not enough space. Good Middlehood drivers are already taking evasive action, based on nothing but instinct. We can never explain how it works to someone just learning to drive. It is the same with our jobs. How do we know what we know? Practice and experience are the real teachers.

> *After more than thirty years as a special education teacher, I often know what's going on with a child, even if I can't document it. It's so frustrating when I know what will help*

a struggling student and can't get services for them because they don't "test" right.

~ Polly T., 55-year-old

On the other hand, despite our experience and instinct, the world and work are changing. Technology is one example of change in the workplace, but every field evolves new theories, new applications, and new circumstances. Are we still really interested in our work? When we were young and beginning our work lives, we were filled with possibilities. We projected our enthusiasm into the future: "We can do this or this. Or let's try this." Do we still do that in Middlehood? Do we still have a zest for learning new things, or are we tired and just want to hang on until we can retire?

This keeping up gets harder as our energy levels change when we hit the middle and later parts of Middlehood. Maybe we start feeling the pull towards retiring at this time. We may still have lots of energy for our work, but if we use up all of our waking hours and enthusiasm at work, we will likely not have much left for our loved ones and friends. On the other hand, if we start to pull our energy and attention away from work, we run the risk of falling behind at our job, which could be disastrous! Remember the old conundrum we used to face as women in the workplace: we have to work twice as hard to prove we are just as good. Bottom line, we have to make choices and figure out our priorities so that we are not perpetually too tired to do anything.

I guess I'm more stingy with my time. Time is precious, especially while I'm still working and trying to balance everything. I want to do everything: I want time for my hobbies, I want to spend time with my grandchild. I'm really picky about everything—even my social things, people I want to be with—is this how I want to spend my time? Time is precious and if somebody is wasting my time, then I don't want to be there.

~ Carol S., 50-year-old

Retirement

The farther along we go through Middlehood, the more often we ask or answer the question, "When are you going to retire?" For some of us, it is an easy answer: as soon as we can afford to! For others, it is more complicated. Why? The complications could be financial, but because our Work, jobs, and careers mean many different things to us, sorting out what really matters could take some time. Although the question seems simple enough, our answer will contain a lifetime of expectations, plans, hopes, and fears.

I recently retired from a long federal public service career. I had wanted to retire for a long time but needed to wait until I qualified for full pension before I could do so. Now I can live every day as if it were a Saturday.

~ Donna S., 55-year-old

By our mid- to late fifties, we need to face other questions about work and retirement because much of our future happiness and contentment depends on our answers. For instance:

- Are we happy with our jobs/careers, or are we still working because we cannot afford to retire?
- Are we willing to keep investing time and energy in our jobs? Do we look for ways to improve and expand our skills, or are we more interested in staying in our comfort zones?

- Do we feel burdened by the responsibility and challenge to keep up with what is new?
- Are we bored with what we have been doing? Do we dream of doing something else? Developing other skills?
- Have we been working for decades and are just tired?
- Do we have health concerns or caretaking responsibilities that make it hard for us to maintain a full-time job?
- Can we ever really retire from our Work?

Most of us have traveled through the last couple of decades without much thought of what retirement means to us. Oh, we might have dreamed of retirement, and in those dreams, we were always free and rich! Or we may have been good planners and saved for years to take a trip or buy a vacation home. But none of those ideas or dreams really says much about how we feel about retiring.

Let's start by looking at some of the reasons that we do or do not want to retire.

Why We Want to Retire

- We are tired of working in a job we do not like and want to be free to do things we love.
- We are short on energy and want more choices about how to use it.
- We have other interests/work possibilities we want to pursue.
- We are sick of working for someone else—their schedule, their rules, a younger boss.
- We feel old, out-of-date, useless, invisible, or overlooked and want out of such a negative, depressing situation.

- We have been waiting/looking forward to the freedom to do what we want to do for a long time and are financially able to handle it.

Why We Do Not Want to or Cannot Retire

- We *love* what we do and do not want to stop.
- We cannot afford to retire. We might want to, but finances will not allow it.
- We are afraid to retire. What will we do? What will our purpose be? How will we spend our time? Does retiring mean we are getting old?
- We did retire but had to return to work because of finances.

Many reasons in the Want to Retire category have direct or implied negativity. One of the first things many of us express when we consider retiring is the feeling that we can finally do "what we want to do." Of course the implication is that we are not doing what we want to do while we are working. That is a bit alarming! Are we waiting to live our lives until we retire? Are we so focused on our jobs that we forget our other dreams? Are we one of the people whose energy drains away for years and then suddenly returns as retiring becomes imminent? Are there things we can do now? Do we have to wait for years? For decades? Things can happen . . .

A friend of mine retired after years in the school system. She and her husband planned to travel and relax. Within a year after she retired, she was diagnosed with cancer and died a year later. I think about that—I know it doesn't happen to everybody, but still it makes me think twice when I keep putting things I want to do off until "later, when I retire and have more time." Maybe all the time I've got is right now!

~ Peggy H., 60-year-old

And for some of us, it is not about the work at all. We may be happy with our jobs and cannot really imagine not working, but we have spent decades setting alarm clocks, planning vacations in two-week blocks, being in rush hour traffic every day, and eating at certain times because we have a constant schedule. We know that dreamy, relaxed feeling that comes over us when we think of a life that runs on our schedules—when we can get up when we are done sleeping, go to bed when we are tired, eat when we are hungry, and dive deeply into projects for as long as we want without having to stop because something else on our planner needs our attention.

For most women, the simple, positive reason to retire is that we are ready to devote more time to the other things we love to do—time with family and friends, traveling, pursuing hobbies, or even launching into another career. Most of us have talents and interests that we do not use in our jobs. We are often astonished when we find out that a coworker is a terrific painter, singer, athlete, scuba diver, or board member of a significant organization. For many of us, retiring is not about withdrawing or going to bed; it is about regrouping in order to begin again.

I love to travel. I started traveling when I was ten years old, and I am still going at sixty-four. I have always wanted to know what was beyond the gate of the yard or what was beyond the end of the road, past where I could see. . . . A lot of things have changed over the years—where I go and how I do things. When I was younger I took more active trips, hiking for a week or two at a time or in remote areas, but I have always been a bit of a wimp. I like coming back to electricity and running, drinkable water. Now that I am retired, I can travel more often, but my body isn't permitting me to do the big treks and mountain climbing that I once did. The state of the world is also presenting limitations as to where I can safely go. But I still want to see what is beyond the fence, beyond the end of the road. Now I go on active trips but with shorter hikes and more emphasis on nature and wildlife and still have adventures, but at a slower pace. I am still enriched by finding new experiences, meeting new people, and learning about different cultures. And I still like coming home to electricity and running water. The curious explorer is still there, but she moves slower and she hopes there will always be a road to explore and see what is beyond.

~ Linda B., 64-year-old

Whether we are filled with anticipation or dread, retiring is one of the most potent external symbols of aging in our society and sets us apart from the majority of adults who are working. How strange it feels! For some, retiring is a relief, and we are happy to be done with the workaday world; but for many of us, happy or not, it is a bit disorienting. Before we retire, we worry about how we will stop caring about everything that has been important to us for so long. Do we just turn everything over to someone else? How will we let go? Of course after we retire, we wonder how we ever had time to work and do everything else we love to do.

Baby boomers are the first generation of women to formally retire in large numbers. There have always been women who worked outside the home or had careers, but many of our mothers did not. So here at this critical life passage, we may have to look to our fathers rather than our mothers as examples. We may find ourselves understanding a lot more about this time in our fathers' lives: the questions of value and purpose with which they struggled. Some of them enjoyed their retirement and finally did many more things they loved, whether hanging out at the coffee shop with friends, fishing, traveling, volunteering, or playing in a band. Others were bored out of their minds and could never seem to find anything to do and (many of our mothers will nod their heads in agreement here) drove our mothers crazy.

Now it is us thinking about retirement, and despite some of the shared feelings with our fathers, retiring now is different from what it was thirty years ago. One of the profound differences is that retirement, to our parents, meant no more working. Once someone received their gold watch, they were done—and they stayed done. They might have had hobbies or volunteered to help with a project or service of some kind, but work, job, career were finished. Not so much anymore. Many of us cannot afford to retire completely, living on retirement savings, pensions, or Social Security. Perhaps we did not seriously start saving money until we were older, or perhaps we did but lost it in financial disaster. Either way, plenty of us are a long way from being ready to retire with any sense of financial security.

Along with financial concerns, consider that the concept of retirement is recent in human history and even today is limited to people in certain income brackets. Not very long ago most people did not retire; they just got old. They worked until they could not anymore, and then someone took care of them. As a society, are we returning to that? Is retiring an idea whose time has come and gone?

For many Middlehood women right now, retiring from a job does not necessarily mean an end to working. We are living longer and finding new venues for our skills or starting entirely new careers in our fifties and sixties. The lines between vocation and avocation are blurring. We are back to the questions we pondered earlier: "What am I doing? What do I want to do?" For some people, the answers are quick and easy: we want to travel, spend time with grandkids, take a class, or even simpler, we just want to rest. But for others, the answers are far more complex, going into deeper realms of spirituality and life purpose. "What is my Work now—the Work of my heart?"

If we are asking that question, we might be ready to step out of the norm, out of a familiar job and into a commitment to our Work that we have never had before. Maybe jobs were just jobs when we were younger, but suddenly, here in Middlehood, we are finding a way to make our job and our Work be the same thing. We may have always worked hard, but imagine spending each day working on something that truly matters to us, something we feel called to do.

How and when we retire or do not retire has a lot to do with who we are as people, as well as our financial circumstances, and Middlehood is where the questions we are asking become particularly important. The decisions that we make about work and retirement are huge, so it is no surprise that we experience mixed feelings: excitement, confusion, fear, and relief. Once we no longer have a regular job, we lose the structure that formed our day-to-day lives for a long time, and we may be surprised by all of the decisions we have to consciously make that used to be automatic. Fully retiring is a big life event, requiring much thought beyond finances. Just like any other life stage change, we will need the support of family and friends as much as we did when we had a baby, got married, or lost a parent.

> *One of the big things I notice as I cut back on work is that I don't need dress-up clothes and makeup anymore—there's no more adorning. I'm becoming more androgynous. It's becoming a new normal. It raises a lot of questions for me about my femininity and identity and how I present myself. I also look forward to going out more—I'm not as tired. I have to choose to socialize, it's more deliberate.*
>
> ~ Kathryn B., 61-year-old

Whether or not we are ready to retire now, we have experiences and perspective from the past *and* energy and plans for the future. Most of us still have twenty, thirty, or more years in front of us, although twenty or thirty years seems much shorter than it did when we were younger. So what are we going to do with all that time?

Once again, if we shape our questions through the Equation for Transformation, we may find helpful insights about where we go from here. It could be interesting to identify the jobs or interests that are ending, the skills and passions we want to begin or continue to develop, and what is calling to us or opening into the future.

Maybe the secret word that sums up what we have learned in Middlehood is *and*. Our elders were right, *and* so were we. Planning for our futures *and* living in the richness of today are what help us create a powerful, joyful Middlehood. We are learning to let go of our past "either/or's" and realizing that one of the most important qualities we need is flexibility. Our day-to-day lives are precious, not just time to hurry or suffer through until we reach our golden years. The real question is, why have we not been living a golden life all along? Most of us will have some regrets at the end of our lives because life just is not long enough to do everything we want to do. But let us make sure those regrets are few and that we have spent the majority of our hours and days doing our Work.

Reflection Questions

- How am I balancing my work life with my personal life in a way that makes me happy?
- What is my real Work? How can I incorporate it into my job or other activities?
- If I could retire right now, what would I do?

CHAPTER 11

Accumulated Wisdom

Owning our story can be hard but not nearly as difficult as spending our lives running from it. Embracing our vulnerabilities is risky but not nearly as dangerous as giving up on love and belonging and joy—the experiences that make us the most vulnerable. Only when we are brave enough to explore the darkness will we discover the infinite power of our light.

~ Brené Brown, *Daring Greatly*

Some people see scars, and it is wounding they remember. To me they are proof of the fact that there is healing.

~ Linda Hogan, *Woman Who Watches Over the World: A Native Memoir*

BY THE TIME WE REACH MIDDLEHOOD, we probably have accumulated quite a collection of photos, memories, out-of-date clothes, friends, extra pounds, funny stories, and stuff, stuff, stuff. Some of these things are precious gifts of getting older, and some are just the leftover clutter and debris from our busy lives. But more than anything, we should pay attention to the wisdom we have gathered—our accumulated wisdom—the lessons and insights we have gleaned from decades of life and experience. This knowledge

212

is not something we read in a book; it is the real-life knowing that comes from having survived heartbreak, disappointment, and loss as well as success, accomplishment, and fulfillment. We know how to see below the surface of things and are not as captivated by bright, shiny baubles as we used to be. We have so much more understanding about what motivates us and about why other people do what they do.

At this time in life . . . a quality (I need) in close friends is the ability to swim in deep waters, to hold ambiguity, to be able to take in the horror of the world and yet balance it with the wonder of the world.

~ Rhea M., 58-year-old

This ability to hold ambiguity is one of the most valuable qualities or skills we acquire as we get older and accumulate more experience. We are less prone to force choices in ourselves and others. We can see both sides of a conflict, hold the ambiguity and understand that there may be value in both positions.

But one of our biggest shocks is our sudden understanding of the ambiguity of aging itself. Two things are happening at the same time, and there is no choosing between them. We are beginning to accept that we are not the same as we used to be and that our life experiences have really changed us. At the same time we know that we *are* the same person we have always been, regardless of how we look on the outside. It is both hilarious and confusing that our children and grandchildren think that we have always been old, no matter how young we are, and our parents will always see us as young, no matter how old we get. Thank heavens for siblings and friends, who see both: the young ones we were *and* the Middlehood ones we have become.

One day when I was close to thirty, I was spending time with my grandmother who was in her early eighties. As we were getting ready to go out to lunch, Nana stared into the mirror while she pulled on her sweater. She peered long and hard at her reflection and then said, "Sometimes when I see myself in the mirror these days, I think, 'Who is that old lady?' because that is not how I feel inside!" I didn't know what to say—what in the world did she mean? Of course she was old! Nana just shrugged and off we went. Now at fifty-seven, I know just what she meant—in a middle-aged sort of way. Sometimes I just stare in the mirror and wonder what happened to my face!

~ 57-year-old

This process is so deeply personal that many of us cannot find words to describe how strange and unsettling it is. We hold what seems fleeting and what seems permanent about who we are, and both are absolutely true. Somehow as we enter Middlehood and pass through these decades, we must continue to deepen our choices about what to keep and what to release. Putting things off when we are young, when it seems like we have forever, is so easy that we accumulate disconnected fragments of old plans and dreams along with real treasure. But now it is vital to do the sorting, to get rid of clutter and fluff so we can focus on what is most important. In the old story of the wise woman and the precious stone, we see that moment of knowing the wisdom of the old woman and the beginning of wisdom in the young traveler.

While she was traveling, an old woman found a beautiful jewel. She put it in her bag and continued her journey. Sometime later she encountered another traveler, a young man, who was hungry and asked her for food. She willingly opened her bag and took out bread to give him. While her bag was open, he saw the jewel and asked her for that instead. Just as willingly, the woman retrieved the stone and gave it to him. Surprised and joyful that she gave it so willingly, the young man left, knowing that the jewel was worth enough to keep him secure and comfortable for the rest of his life. The woman continued on. Several days later, the young man found her again and returned the stone. He told her that he had given it a lot of thought and decided he didn't want the stone after all, even though he knew how valuable it was. Rather, he hoped she would share what she had within her that allowed her to give him the stone in the first place.

Many things from our past fall away gently, and other things—not so much. There are those moments when we may realize that an old pattern or activity has faded, and we did not even notice. Other times we face wrenching choices, peeling our fingers off a way of life that is no longer appropriate or possible yet is hell to release. This process is likely to stir up every emotion we can imagine: laughter, surprise, sadness, fear, and hurt. Here comes that need for the Equation for Transformation again! The transformations that happen during life stage changes are not punishments, but opportunities to create the space and energy to welcome what is fresh and new, and to gently and lovingly release what we have outgrown.

Years ago, late author Cynthia Henry wrote a personal myth that described her journey through some of the struggles of her life. In her story, she described the life of a cat that had lost her purr by giving up parts of herself trying to please others. Over the years, the cat lost so many bits and pieces that she was left with a life that felt flat and gray. Many of us know that feeling: we have lost touch with the core of who we are, given away pieces of ourselves, hoping that we will have a life of ease and happiness. It never works, but most of us have learned that lesson *after* we have wasted precious time trying to make it work. In the story, the cat finally realizes that she still has memories and treasures from her whole life collected in a beautiful tapestry bag. We tap our real power when we realize that, just like the cat, we each have such a bag filled with all that is most precious to us. No matter how tattered and torn we get, the treasures we carry can be made new again, and we too will find our purr hidden there.

This is the real lesson of aging, the real power of accumulated wisdom. We each learn many specifics, but the overriding theme—for everyone—is to learn to believe in ourselves and respect the truth of who we are. Some of us were able to make this commitment when we were young, and our present lives are a reflection of that choice. For others of us, *now* is the time to say, "I will do whatever is necessary to walk my path." Doing so gives us a way to step back and observe ourselves. Maybe we have been too tired or stretched too thin to do what we know we should be doing. Maybe we have been afraid of what others might think of us. There are many reasons why we may not have lived up to our truest self, but here in Middlehood, we are brave enough to see our truth, and now is the time to do this work for ourselves. How did our wise elders and role models do it? They did it the same way we are doing it: by losing touch and then finding our way again; by making choices, hard or easy, and living with the results. It is a process, like everything in life: two steps forward, one step back.

> *I am no longer afraid to be who I am, to express my thoughts and emotions and to enjoy all life has to offer.*
>
> ~ Susan McC., 58-year-old

The bag of memories and treasures we each carry and the purr emanating from the deepest part of us are signs that we are on our path. If we have been trying to embody beliefs we inherited that do not ring true, it is time to put them down—no shame, no blame. If we have been pretzels, twisting this way and that to please someone else, that time is over. If our homes and lives have been filled with clutter and unimportant things, we may find that now it is easier to create more space. Everything that does not feed us—outdated ideas and beliefs in particular—sucks away energy, clarity, and purpose. What we need is not judgment of ourselves but the courage to let go of what is not ours and to deeply commit ourselves to what is ours. We can use the steps of the Equation for Transformation—completing what is passing, being patient in the in-between place, and getting ready for the new—for questions and challenges, large and small. This process clarifies our core strengths, beliefs, and values. We have much work to do in this middle phase of life, making sense of our pasts and making peace with our inconsistencies. We will build our futures on those choices, but any dissonance and disharmony will continue to challenge us until we find ways to face our contradictions.

I am generally happy and positive. I believe if you give good, you get good. I have had a lot of challenges in my life, but I have never been caught up in the "why me," but rather in having faith that there is a reason for everything, and if I just hang in there, the silver lining will appear.

~ Deb McB., 50-year-old

Whether we believe in free will, karma, or predestination, most of us have noticed by now the patterns or themes operating throughout our lives. Some of those patterns are a clear result of our choices, while others have more to do with circumstances and our responses to them. Some themes are so ingrained that we wonder if they are the result of genetics or some other inherent quality. Truly, life always seems to be a combination of these patterns and pure surprise. In fact, it may be that our themes and what we learn from them can really help when life throws us a big curve.

> *Be sweetly stubborn. Just do the next right thing, however large or small. Movement turns into momentum. Just keep moving in what feels like an honorable direction.*
>
> ~ Cindy L., 49-year-old

As we get older, we begin to accept the repetitive nature of these challenges and issues that make up our life journey. Issues may keep surfacing in different guises or in different circumstances or particulars, but they feel familiar. We need tools to help us cope, and that is what we spend our whole lives learning. Just as in a book we read over and over, we find something new, something deeper each time. This is how we heal and grow in our own particular style. Every time we face one of our familiar challenges, we learn more about how and where we break down and what we need to strengthen, so they have less power over us. This deepening knowledge, gained through time and experience, is one of the blessings of growing older. We can feel its gift as some of our old fears and furies begin to fade, and a certain calm acceptance takes their place.

> *I am very spiritual and I find a lot of fulfillment exploring that area of my life. My current operating philosophy of life is that it is not about weathering the storm, but it's about learning to dance in the rain.*
>
> ~ 56-year-old

Spirituality and Values

For some of us, our life paths have deep roots in an organized faith or traditional religion. Others have a more eclectic or undefined sense of spirituality and have followed a winding path of exploration. And many of us do not seek a connection to a higher power at all, but rather over time have built strong ethics and values that provide the guidance we need to make choices in our lives.

Spirituality keeps my path forward and brings me back on course when I stray. It gives me the strength and the courage to forge on, even when I am afraid of the unknown. It gives me peace when the world is a storm all around me.

~ Stacy H., 43-year-old

Whatever path we follow, we should rely on it to negotiate the twists and turns of our Middlehood years and to help us replenish and regenerate. If the path seems too difficult, we might shift over to a different one that seems easier or better. We have all experienced that grass-is-greener feeling and perhaps tried abandoning what we knew at one time. If we did that without a sense of integrity, we may have wound up more confused.

We have learned some lessons the hard way and need to apply them to the changing waters of Middlehood. This tumultuous time is full of potential, if we are brave and determined. The new lessons we learn and new tools and insights we acquire must lead to coherency. For example, if we rush from one religion or spiritual path to another or take workshop after workshop, hoping to find something or someone to give us "the answer," we are doomed to chaos. On the other hand, if we approach our search with honesty and clarity about who we are and what we need help with, we may find assistance, peace, and guidance by committing to another spiritual practice or discipline. Sometimes it is not a new practice we need but a deeper commitment to the path we have always walked. Maybe we missed a step or got sidetracked and stepped off our path, and the real work is to find our way back.

> *My purpose in life is to try to go by instinct, intention, heart, and spirit. I sometimes give it over to dreams. And I seek counsel from friends of heart.*
>
> ~ Cherie S., 57-year-old

We need to ask ourselves, what do I need to feel calm, safe, whole, open, loving, or connected to the spirit? How can I live my life with honesty, generosity, and truth? Some helpful ways to explore may be meditation, exercise, therapy, diet, spiritual practice, creative practice or service—an honest assessment of our answers will guide us to choose what is right.

We will never walk around a corner and find the answers, but if we operate with our true spirit and instinct, we will not stray far from our path. We continue to learn how to be in our own space in the midst of all the external stimulation.

> *I was feeling stressed and overwhelmed with too much going on in my life, so I decided to go for a hike. That's always been one of the best ways for me to relax and think about my life. I got up to my favorite spot —my "quiet spot" off the trail—and tucked myself in behind a big boulder where nobody could see me. While I was sitting there quietly meditating and praying, a guy on a mountain bike stopped right in front of my boulder and started cussing a blue streak about his bicycle. At first I got upset. Isn't there any place I can go to find some peace and quiet? And then I realized how ridiculous it was and had to laugh.*
>
> ~ 52-year-old

In spite of the clarity and experience we achieve, many of us continue to grapple with questions we have faced time after time throughout our lives. A common question is, how do we balance our needs with the needs of others? We will continue to ask variations of this question on a regular basis. How do we maintain our optimism, hope, and goals, and also maintain loving relationships with family and friends? How do we replenish and refill when so many other people and situations demand our attention? How do we pour energy and creativity into our Work and jobs when we are divided into multiple roles every day? And what happens when we lose our balance and end up depleted, sad, judgmental, or even depressed? Does it help to close off emotionally in an attempt to protect ourselves? Not usually. If we have tried that in the past, we likely found that we ended up closing off to sustenance as well.

We need to have grace. There's no grace for each other. We have a responsibility when we see opportunities to mentor. To help and mentor women our own ages.

~ Lucinda L., 53-year-old

We can find consistent guidance on these questions no matter which spiritual tradition or life path we follow. The essence of this guiding wisdom is the principle of reciprocity: what we give is what we will receive, and for everything we receive, we need to give something back. If we need unconditional love, acceptance, patience, respect, fairness, openness, support, or kindness, then that is what we need to offer others. Our hearts are often the first place where we realize that what we do for others is also good for us, but it easily carries out into the world. Our well-being and the well-being of those around us are very interrelated. If it seems that everyone around us is begging, "Help me! Pay attention to me!" or even "Leave me alone!" Are those our cries too? Remember that within the principle of reciprocity is a reminder to make sure we are also getting what we need. If not, then we must find our way to balance—for us and for others.

Our paths are illuminated when we open up to ourselves and each other. Our ability to see the sadness and longing and needs in others helps us to see them in ourselves, and vice versa. If we learn how to care for ourselves, we will be better able to care for others— our families and our communities. If we practice compassion for others, we need to practice compassion for ourselves as well. Back and forth, back and forth the pendulum swings, with powerful regularity: what we are searching for, others search for too. As we deepen our capacity to love and care, we will find more love and care around us.

I truly believe in responsibility and accountability, that every action has a consequence, and that by making choices, we will invoke the appropriate consequence (we just may not agree with "appropriate" at the time). I believe in honesty, openness, and in doing unto others. It's okay not to win at everything, and when you don't win, it's perfectly okay that someone else does. I also believe that everything happens for a purpose, although sometimes that purpose isn't clear to us.

~ Sandy R., 58-year-old

The issues we struggle with are part of our path, but we carry many of them differently than we did when we were younger. Some we carry more lightly—perhaps we have gained more mercy and understanding for ourselves and others or more patience with what it takes to make real change. At the same time, other issues may feel heavier because they are time-related, not just theoretical anymore: questions of death and dying, aging or loss. We think of flexibility as mostly physical (it really was easier to touch our toes when we were younger), but we need emotional and spiritual flexibility too.

> *My confidence is wonderful. I never felt confident like this until I turned forty. I think my lack of confidence was my biggest weakness in my younger years. It prevented me from doing things I dreamed of. Now I know I can do about anything—but now, I feel like I'm running out of time. The best thing is I finally love me! I think I'm great! I'm passionate about being a good role model for kids. I am incorporating my passion into my everyday life. I'm not a very spiritual person. I believe in God, but I have my own relationship with him, a relationship not defined by a church or person. My spirituality is just me doing the right thing.*
>
> ~ Julie A., 43-year-old

We are looking for balance in many aspects of our lives: between activity and rest, our needs and the needs of others, what we want to do and what we need to do. We can choose from a variety of techniques to help us, but that is what they are: techniques. The essence of what we have always sought is the calmness that comes with the balance. We have known that balance at various times in our lives, and perhaps now, more than ever before, we know how important it is to find our way into that balance. As soon as we find it we open up—our hearts open, our breathing deepens, and our bodies come into alignment. Opening up helps us let go of judgments and fears and the stress we perpetually carry. Even a brief time is restful and healing. We might think that closing ourselves off is the best way to protect ourselves, but it only leaves us more vulnerable. When we get tired, we long for something different, something that is not ours. Instead, we need to discover our way to replenish and regenerate. Our path should help us, but if it does not, we need to ask questions and be honest with our answers.

- Is this method still a viable way for me to find balance, or is it out-of- date?
- Is it true to the core of who I am, or did I inherit it from someone else, never really questioning whether it was right for me?
- If it is a good path for me, am I committed to going deeper and learning more, even when life is at its most challenging?
- If this path is no longer working for me, am I able to let go and try something new?

Strangely enough, we sometimes find the guidance we need relatively quickly but then doubt the answers because they came too easily. Aren't we supposed to struggle more? Those who have studied dance, or a sport or martial art that blends grace and strength, know how deeply that belief is ingrained. We sweat, pushed, and ground through practice after practice, gaining skills, but were often frustrated by the difficulty. And then one day, we just gave up and—we got it. It happened—effortlessly, almost like magic. Practice made it possible, but the secret was not in the pushing, it was in the letting go: of too much thinking, self-judgment, anger, or desperation. The moment we were able to relax and let the energy flow through us, everything came together, and it seemed easy.

I will never forget an aikido class I took years ago. We were practicing a particular move—holding our partner's arm, putting pressure on their shoulder, and trying to force them to the mat. Our instructor told us to resist as hard as we could when our partner was trying to accomplish the move. I remember when it was my turn to try the move, I struggled and struggled to force my partner to the mat. She was about my size and weight, so we were equally matched in terms of strength, and nothing I did seemed to work. We spun around in circles as I pushed and she resisted. After watching us for a little while, my teacher came over and touched my hands. "All you have to do is hold this position and think down." He took his hands away, and I looked at him like he was crazy! Feeling slightly ridiculous, I put my hands back in position, stared at the mat, and thought "down" as hard as I could. Instantly, my partner was flat on the mat. I laughed: "Oh, come on. I didn't even do anything. You just fell down to make me feel better!" "Nope," she said, "the minute you got it, there was nowhere to go but down." I didn't believe her until we switched roles, and I felt it the moment she aligned her position and focus—there really was nowhere to go but down!

~ 57-year-old

For many of us, the hard part is not searching for guidance and insight; it is trusting and implementing what we learn and figuring out how to apply it in our lives. We need to trust the answers and start asking, how do I use that? Sometimes we learn what we need to know in steps, sometimes it comes as a whole piece, but either way, we do not have to wait years and years to see results. We can feel it as our energy increases. We can see it in somebody's eyes when we step into clarity and calmness. We can feel it when we are able to do our Work. Like so many things, what is good and right for us is not necessarily easy. Sometimes it is just plain hard work—but it is good work.

It just takes us half a lifetime to integrate the wisdom that our life experiences have carved into our soul.

~ Karla M., 56-year-old

Inspiration and Guidance from Others

Who or what inspired us when we were young? Was it a person? A book? A movie? A piece of music or a dream we had? In those youthful images we can find the seeds of our lifelong curiosity, passions, and commitment to life. Those early callings may have carried with them the power to help us make decisions and face challenges when we were young. How do those images live in us now? We may still love sports even though we never became a professional athlete: do we still feel like we are flying when we go for a run, or do we coach a kids' team? Did we imagine ourselves singing at Carnegie Hall or heading up a rock band when we were teens? How do we enjoy music now: church choir or quiet morning piano time? Were we always rescuing injured or baby animals as little girls? Most of us who did are probably not veterinarians today, but maybe we own a rescue horse or a beloved dog from the pound. As we reexplore our life path during Middlehood, searching for the knowledge and wisdom we have gained over the years, we may be drawn to those early images of ourselves. In them could be insights to strengths we now possess or clues to the yearning we feel for missing pieces of the puzzle.

Sometimes inspiration has come from people. Our heroes, mentors, or role models can be anybody in our lives: a family member, friend, or professional, a teacher, coach, boss, or coworker. The stories of their impact on our lives can come from a long, deep relationship or from a chance encounter.

I lived in a small Vermont town, and our elementary school had grades one through eight in three rooms. One winter afternoon, when I was in second grade, my teacher announced that we were going to have a special art teacher visit us. I was excited for the break in routine because it was such a typical grey afternoon: grey sky, my teacher had on grey flannel, the boys had on grey plaid flannel, and the slate board was grey. At 1:30 p.m. our door opened, and a walking rainbow beamed into our room—the art teacher had arrived! I had never seen anyone like her. She was Navajo and nothing about her was grey! She had wispy silver hair in a bun on terra cotta skin. Her blouse was dark-blue velvet with silver and turquoise jewelry everywhere. Her skirt was a breeze of green velvet swirls and pleats. Her boots were a soft brown and did not make noise when she walked. When she looked at you, she "saw" you and heard what you said. She was amazing. After class she sent a note home to my mother asking if I could be allowed to attend after-school art classes—she thought I showed promise. I spent many late afternoons with her and now that I look back on it, I realize that the time with her was as important to me as the art.

~ Rhona F., 53-year-old

When I was a young woman, I had the incredible gift of meeting and working with a powerful and wise woman named Lucille Kinlein. She is a healthcare practitioner and counselor with a rare and unique ability to help people see more deeply into themselves in order to find their way through confusion and back to clarity. I went to see her off and on during a tumultuous time in my life and still today, twenty-eight years later, remember and pass on some of her wisdom.

Once I had a job that I was tired of but felt I couldn't leave. I talked long and often about it, always focused on what I didn't like and what I thought was wrong with it. Lucille was a deep and patient listener, but one day she gently said to me, "Your job is not a bad job. It's a perfectly fine job; it just isn't what you want right now. You keep trying to make it bad, so you can leave it. You don't need to do that. The choice between good and bad is what we learn as children. You already know how to choose between what is good for you and what is bad for you. Now the choice is between good and better. You never have to stay with something bad again; now your choices are always between something good and something better. Make your choice based on that."

Another time I was feeling like my life was going nowhere. In an attempt to free up my thinking, Lucille asked me to close my eyes and imagine the perfect day. I closed my eyes and waited for an image to appear. Nothing! Completely blank! "Okay," Lucille said, "Try this. Tell me what you want." Immediately, pictures and feelings began to pour out of me. I started talking with passion and emotion about everything I wanted in my life. After a few minutes, I ran out of words and sat silently with my heart pounding from the intensity of my feelings. Quietly, Lucille leaned over, put her hand on my knee, and said, "Then I propose to you that the things you want most in the world are the very things you have to give." My reaction was so sudden and so intense that I felt like she had slapped me on the back of the head. She continued, "There is nothing in the world that you know better than the things you want the most—you know how they feel, how they smell, you know the touch of them. If you want love, then give love. If you want peace, then find a way to give peace. If you can do this, you will get what you want."

It all came down to getting unstuck. "Life is movement," she would say. "When you feel stuck, find out what is moving in your life. It could be anything, large or small. Where there is motion, there's energy, and where there is energy, you can direct it and build on it. There's always something in us that is moving."

One day I was telling Lucille about going through bookstores and libraries looking for a book—a certain kind of book. I didn't know the name of it or what it was about exactly, but I had a feeling about it, and I knew I'd know it when I saw it. I'd been looking for a long time and was frustrated because I couldn't find it. Lucille smiled kindly and said, "That's because you haven't written it yet. The book you're looking for is the one you are going to write." Stunned, I said, "I guess I'd like to write a book, but I don't know if I ever will." Lucille smiled again and said, "You will; it's 'when,' not 'if.' Talk about it that way because when you do, I'll want to read it."

~ Jane T., 58-year-old

Many of our mothers are heroes to us because of the sacrifices they made for their children and others.

My Momma, Allene Marie Geha, was amazing, to put it mildly. She gave birth to twelve children and went through the incredible pain of losing her twenty-one-year-old daughter to an extended illness. Over the years her sacrifices and strength have been lessons of love for my Papa, siblings, thirty grandchildren, two great-grandchildren, and me. There were times when there wasn't enough food at a family meal, and she would give her portion to one of us. It's hard for some people to imagine the daily cleaning, cooking, and upkeep of our home with twelve children always underfoot, undoing what she had just done. Despite the challenges, she chose to be a funny, kind, patient, and loving woman, and somehow, in spite of it all, she didn't lose her mind!

~ Nancy G., 53-year-old

In Middlehood, we have already lived through some hard times and found lessons and learning from those experiences. Our family and friends have always held and encouraged us when we were lost and overwhelmed, and we may still find inspiration in spiritual beliefs or teachers. But where do we find new sources of motivation? What or who inspires us now? What helps us find the inner strength to carry on when life challenges us? The answers to these questions may offer rich, new opportunities for exploration.

From Inspiration to Action

Whatever our source of inspiration, how do we turn that inspiration into action? It is easy to walk away from a workshop or presentation fired up and anxious to make changes. Does that energy last more than a day? Can we use that energy to take action on behalf of ourselves and others? After a particularly loving and supportive conversation with a family member or friend, are we still feeling open and brave a week later? As Middlehood women, we have been through many cycles of New Year's resolutions. We are not beginners in the process of making a conscious change in our lives. We have watched ourselves lose our good intentions in the hectic hubbub of our daily lives many times. But at other times we have been ready to make changes, and we did. We left a bad relationship, went back to school, quit smoking, lost weight, learned something new, got a great job, or fulfilled a lifelong dream.

How did we do it? Accumulated knowledge and wisdom about ourselves and how we work is vital. When we are honest with ourselves, we know what has worked and what has not. We know that wishful thinking with no commitment does not make definitive change, but hope and a clear vision of where we want to be really helps us reach our goals. We know that negativity and fear can at best be only a call to change, not a long-term path. And maybe, on a deep level, we finally understand that loving ourselves into changing works much better than beating ourselves up for being a failure. In this more confident place, turning to loved ones for help with our choices or seeking professional help feels relatively easy. We are clear that it is help we are looking for, not someone to tell us what to do. Woe unto anyone who tries to boss around a Middlehood woman!

Every woman has her own recommendation for how to make profound and lasting change in her life. In writing this book, we asked many women for their best advice, and we found that most of the individual suggestions boiled down to a few basic ideas:

- Start with one thing, even something small, that makes your life better.
- Hang around with positive people.
- Pray.
- Spend time with people who love and believe in you.
- Laugh often, hard and loud.
- Stay focused on what you want.
- Take it a step at a time.

As Lucille said, find movement and energy and then build on them. Anything that rouses our passion, excitement, anticipation, or joy could be the first step. Any step we take towards our dreams and loves can be a doorway into the circle of who we are, and all doorways lead into the same circle.

Inspiring Others

Here we are halfway up the mountain in Middlehood, and it is important to pay close attention to our growth and the trail in front of us, but—it is also time for us to turn around and see the line of younger people coming behind us, following our lights. If we are mothers, we already know the feeling of children watching us, learning from us—even when we would rather they did not! But now it is not only our kids, and stunningly, it is not even only kids! When in the world did we get old enough to have young adults watching us?

Somewhere in the last decade or two, we have stopped thinking of ourselves as only recipients, wanting a mentor, teacher, or elder to show us the way. We now assume authority in our own right. We will always need experts to teach us what we want to learn, but by the time we hit our forties, we have confidence in what we know.

The time has come when we need to see *ourselves* as guides and mentors in our wider communities. To do that, we have to accept ourselves as Middlehood women, no longer young. This moment sneaks up on many of us and can be emotionally tricky.

It is hard to deal with the feeling of losing our momentum: everything is changing, and we might not be happy about some of those changes. We see ourselves getting older and may need to face the unattractive quality of jealousy that we feel towards younger women. At work, for instance, we have younger bosses and see younger people growing in skills, becoming better equipped to do what we have been doing. We see younger women in early stages of adult life—new careers, new relationships, new babies—and we may long for that feeling of excitement, passion, and newness again. Now instead of feeling fresh and on the brink of new possibilities, we feel disoriented and lost because we are not those young people anymore.

The Equation for Transformation can help us here. We have to let go of old ways of seeing ourselves and take hold of some new ways. First, we have to own up to the fact that we miss some things from our youth. We think fondly of the energy and bodies we had years ago, of everything we looked forward to in happy anticipation. It is hard to put down those feelings and images of ourselves because they were a precious part of who we were and how we came to be who we are now.

None of us are immune to feeling jealous of younger women and longing for the days of our youth, but the only antidote to those feelings is to root deeply in the truth of our lives *now* and focus on the gifts that come at this time in our lives. Once again, we have to release what has passed—honor that time, then bless it and let it go. Only then can we make the space to focus on the new experiences and opportunities of now.

The next steps we take require a great deal of courage, because nothing in our culture supports this process. We must do it for ourselves and for each other. Right here, right now is when we must learn about the other gifts we have to give. One of those gifts is supporting younger people and each other. That is the remedy for jealousy: gratitude, truth, and encouraging others.

Peter Pan has no place in a conscious woman's path through Middlehood. We are not going to stay young no matter what we do; rather, what most of us want is to stay vital and fresh. One of the surest ways is to build on our own strength and vitality and then share it with others. Here is the power of reciprocity again: we will find ourselves renewed as well. Those of us who are mothers and grandmothers know the natural flow of reciprocity with our children and grandchildren, but we may also find this process in the wider society. Whether we do that in our jobs or Work, through volunteering or activism, in our neighborhood or in another country, we have knowledge and experience to share, as well as new experiences and friendships to gain.

One of the treasures of this time in our lives is the amazing epiphany we experience: that we are *all* on this journey up the mountain. As children and young women, we may have felt a great gulf between our lives and priorities and those of our parents and grandparents. It may have seemed that they did not understand us or really know what we were going through. With the gift of hindsight, we now shake our heads and even laugh as we hear our mother's voice come out of us—over and over and over. Or when our teen lashes out with the familiar, "You just don't understand!" and we realize that we *do* understand, we just do not agree. Or maybe we know better now. Perhaps we used to think that people who live in cultures and circumstances far different from ours share nothing with us, their lives too different to find much common ground. Nowadays, we know that is just not the case. The farther up the mountain we go, the more easily we can stretch ourselves to find that common ground and shared humanity. As more and more of the trail unwinds behind us, we are able to see our place in the beauty of the long ribbon of lights. We have to laugh at the irony that, as we get older and younger people see us as more separated and out of step with the world, we know ourselves to be more connected.

An incredible gift comes with our growing awareness that each person's story is both unique and universal. Each human life around us is colored by love and fear, experience and dreams. Our life experiences have taught us that we can best assist and mentor another person by supporting their efforts and helping them to realize their gifts. Their lives are not ours, and even though we may think we know best for someone else, we have learned the hard way that we do not.

> *I like that I care deeply about people, that I can reach out to them in their place of pain and aloneness because I've been there, and empathize.*
>
> ~ Heidi R., 58-year-old

Encouraging young people to be safe, healthy, and true to themselves is a great place to start. When they are ready, we can help them discover the tools they need to accomplish what they want to do. We know for a fact that we cannot *tell* anyone what to do and hope to have a good effect. In fact, when we feel frustrated that no one seems to listen to us anymore, the other side of the question is, are *we* listening? Just because something feels right to us does not mean that it is right for someone else or appropriate in a given situation. Luckily, we are much smarter about choosing our battles these days. We have solid ground beneath us and the courage to stand up for important issues and let the small things go. In truth, we have real wisdom within us.

The images in the story of the wise woman and the precious stone are powerful. As we travel through our lives, discovering treasures in unexpected places enriches us. Like the young traveler, when we were young, we first looked to older people for sustenance and assistance. Now more and more, we look for the shared qualities and the connections between ourselves and others.

The secret to a life filled with satisfaction, excitement, and creativity is simple: we have to change. We cannot stay the same; even if we try, it is not possible. Our bodies will continue to change, and the world around us is changing as well. There is just no stopping it. So are we the first to discover this great unknown truth? Of course not. It is a bit of accumulated wisdom that starts getting clear here in Middlehood. Far more than when we were young, we now make conscious decisions about how we will deal with constant change. When we were young, we may have changed jobs, partners, or living situations on a regular basis. We tried things, experimented, and took other people's suggestions while we figured out what was truly ours. Now we are more judicious about our choices because we have so much more information about ourselves. We have already tried and failed or tried and succeeded many times, but—here is the trick—we must not cling to how things used to be. We need to choose and know why we are choosing. Here the knowledge and wisdom we have gathered comes into play. Some things in our lives are simply no longer negotiable, but many, many things are fair game for expanding, learning, or trying. This is the secret of the elders we know who have a sparkle in their eyes and love life every day.

My friend Jill is eighty-six years old and a great gardener. I'm a big gardener too, and sometimes I tell her something I've learned from my garden that she doesn't know, and she gets so excited! I always think, "How can I be teaching her something about gardening? She's been gardening almost as long as I've been alive!" Then I realize she's delighted to learn something new. She's open and curious—that's her secret. In thirty years, I want to be just like that—excited and interested in life, not just settling for safety and routine. Like Jill, I want a life that's still alive!

~ Jane T., 52-year-old

Jill's message is simple and clear: stay open and stay interested in life. We have to be willing to try new things, meet new people, and learn something new. To do that, we must put aside our pride and learn from younger people or people who are utterly unlike us. If we do the same things over and over, we will stagnate. Stagnation starts early, so we may have to throw a wrench into our own works to keep ourselves moving forward.

My mother's neighbor Sadie was ninety-two years old and still lived alone in her own home. She was physically and mentally very sharp and capably took care of herself. Nevertheless, my middle-aged mom stopped by every so often to check on her and see if Sadie needed assistance with anything. One day, Mom stepped into Sadie's house only to hear "horrible" heavy metal rock music blaring from the TV in the next room. "Sadie!" she exclaimed, "what in the world are you watching?" "MTV," Sadie serenely replied. "I watch it every week." "Do you like it?" asked my mother, incredulous. "Not really," Sadie admitted. "But you know, dear, you must keep up with the young! If you lose touch with what the young people are doing, you soon get left behind".

~ Tally F., 53-year-old

We know there is no going back, and the truth is, there is really no standing still either. Life keeps moving and changing, and so do we. Take a step and breathe . . . take a step and breathe . . .

The question is, are we going to *live* the second half of our lives with passion, creativity, excitement, and humor? If we want that, then we have to make decisions and take action now to ensure that we have the flexibility to face whatever surprises life has in store for us. Will a health challenge change our ways of doing things? Or will a financial upset leave us without resources we depended on? Wisdom traditions from around the world tell us the same thing: we cannot always control what happens to us, but we always have something to say about how we respond. The freedom we are always looking for is not a life without any problems or challenges, because such a thing is not possible. Rather, the freedom comes from the knowledge that nothing can take away our ability to choose our response to whatever happens.

Are we inspiring to others? We should be. We should inspire our children and grandchildren, students, family, friends, and community to love their lives, no matter how old they are; to keep making a difference in the world; to live lives of authenticity, courage, love, truth, compassion and service. We *know* how hard life can be. Are we helping others along the way as people helped us?

We have learned many profound lessons through the years. Some came at a terrible price: the loss of a loved one or of a deeply cherished dream. We have been or we have known others absolutely crushed by pain and suffering, but we have also seen people survive and carry on. And we have seen people rise from the ashes of devastating circumstances and grow in fresh new ways. We know that not all clouds have a silver lining and not all garbage hides a treasure within. Some things in life are the very pile of stinking garbage they appear to be, and no amount of philosophizing can change that. But we have the power to turn that pile of garbage into compost and grow something new: flowers, food, or a new life.

Now in my sixties, I realize that all through my life, every choice I made limited or diminished the number of my future choices. But now I can change that. I can decide if I'm going to keep narrowing my options until I die, or I can step back, let go of my old ways of doing things, and start widening my possibilities again. I want my life to have an hourglass shape.

~ Kath B., 61-year-old

Here in this time of balance between the past and the future is where everything we were and everything we hope to be live within our reach. We have watched past news events from our lives become history, and the household items and toys we grew up with are now antiques! But we know for a fact that not only fashion and style but also ideas recycle and evolve. Our job is to keep running (on a good day) or hobbling along as best we can (on a more challenging day) down the paths of possibilities, keeping our hearts full of gratitude. Remember the old play on words: even if sometimes we feel like we are going nowhere, we are now here! It is still true. We are not who we were, we are not who we are going to be, but—are we who we want to be?

You know what I love about this time in my life? I get to make my own decisions...I enjoy life... I want to learn and explore so much... I enjoy all kinds of people... I enjoy seeing animals in the wild... I love to fish, be outside, and walk in the wilderness... I enjoy my friends and family, but I value them more than I ever have.

~ Carol N., 60-year-old

Are we still sitting around waiting for someone to tell us what to do? Not likely. Or someone to save us? No, that never worked before. Do we still think that someone else knows us better than we do? No, the days of looking outside of ourselves for answers are over. There are people we can learn from, and there are people we can teach, but no one knows which road we should follow. Incredibly, as the brilliant poet June Jordan writes, "We are the ones we have been waiting for."

Reflection Questions

- What has become my accumulated wisdom, the most important things I have to offer from my life experience and skills?
- Is something from the past holding me back: an old choice, accident, or loss? How can I apply the Equation for Transformation to this situation and move on?
- What am I most grateful for? What has most surprised me?

CHAPTER 12

Women and Mountains III

Do you really want to look back on your life and see how wonderful it could have been had you not been afraid to live it?

~ Caroline Myss

When there is a great disappointment, we don't know if that's the end of the story. It may be just the beginning of a great adventure.

~ Pema Chödrön

LIFE AS A MOUNTAIN . . . SO HOW does a Middlehood woman climb a mountain? We don't usually bound along like mountain goats anymore, although we may be quite strong. We almost never forget to bring water and a first-aid kit, because planning and preparation are second nature now. And despite the fact that climbing sometimes requires a lot of huffing and puffing just to keep going, we know that at other times, we will dance our way up the trail! We are, as we have always been, a mixture of strength and weakness, confidence and fear, determination and hesitation.

So why is it that we have that little voice, the sneaky little voice that starts whining in our ear? "Oh, I can't do that—it's too hard."

Or "I'm getting kind of old for that." Or "I'd better not try that; I might hurt myself." When did that start? Did we turn an ankle on a hike? Feel less confident trying to get our balance? Develop a chronic pain in a joint from wear and tear? Of course, any of these things can and do happen to younger people, but we did not expect them when we were younger, so we were not afraid. Injury and disaster always took us by surprise!

Where does this fearfulness come from now? Some comes from our experiences. For instance, we know that in Middlehood we take much longer to heal than we used to, but we may also be reacting to the changes our bodies are going through. We may not yet have adapted to those changes and are in that strange time when our bodies do not feel trustworthy or familiar anymore. Many of us also feel a tremendous sense of grief for the strength and beauty we feel we are losing. Are we trying to protect ourselves from this sadness by not testing ourselves anymore?

Some of us have lived our whole lives with chronic illness or physical challenges, and all of us are beginning to feel new physical limitations. So what do we do when our bodies cannot always go where our spirits would? Do we worry and fret about possible dangers or problems and scare ourselves right out of taking risks, or do we hear our fear as a clarion call to get busy finding new ways to accomplish our dreams?

Walking in Nepal by Jane Treat and Susan McCarn Gambill

One day I sat in the shadow of an old oak tree in a park in Washington, DC, and listened to my friend Susan tell her story of trekking in Nepal—a lifelong dream come true of walking high in the Himalayas. It would have been a challenging experience for anyone, but for Susan, a woman approaching Middlehood with chronic health problems, just the decision to travel to Nepal was a major accomplishment. Susan explains, "In a way, the journey itself was the destination—where, in order to even attempt it, I had to make choices to prepare and care for myself. I had many fears. For instance, I was afraid to spend my limited money just to fulfill a dream, and I was also afraid that my body couldn't take the challenges. But I decided I had to try. . . . The remarkable part of the story to me has to do with actually doing it, despite many obvious barriers. I had wanted to trek for years, but because of severe foot problems, I thought I couldn't. How did I change my mind? Simple: one day it occurred to me that if I could walk at all, I might as well be walking in Nepal! So I arranged to set off."

Following a three-month retreat with renowned Buddhist teacher Thich Nhat Hanh, Susan and her friend Linda planned their trek. In addition to feeling incapacitating pain in her feet if she walks more than a few miles, Susan is also allergic to cold, which gives her asthma and hives. Multiple food allergies limit what she can eat. Despite these limitations, Susan and Linda arrived in Nepal and planned a fourteen-day journey through one of the few remaining Buddhist regions of the country near the Tibetan border. They hired two men as guides and caretakers, and mapped out a very precise itinerary through an area with many villages so that Susan would not have to carry anything, and she could be evacuated easily if her feet gave out. Unlike the other westerners they encountered, who trekked for sport and covered many miles in a day, Linda and Susan planned for shorter days, only four to six hours, and a total distance of sixty to seventy miles over the two weeks. Susan brought medicine for the hives and asthma, and special salts to soak her feet. Summing up her preparations and plans, Susan put it this way: "My body, like my soul, is this extraordinary mix of fragility and strength. I am so robust and energetic, and I have many chronic health problems. I am free as long as I remember and attend to them, accept them, and then do what I want to do anyway."

On their very first day of traveling, the earliest stretch of walking was over a riverbed of fist-sized rocks. The uneven and unstable surface triggered Susan's foot problems, and within forty-five minutes of starting, she was in excruciating pain. Shocked to have so much pain at the very beginning of the trip, Susan was hesitant to even tell her companions. When she finally did, they graciously stopped and massaged her feet. Soon after, the rocks ended and her feet were fine.

They came to an ancient village perched high in the mountains on the second evening. Fascinated by the land and the people of the area, who were mostly of Tibetan descent, Susan and Linda visited the local monastery. Later, they quietly watched goats come in from the field, heard an avalanche, and then over dinner, listened to their guide tell the story of his sister's life as a village outcast. They planned to hike to a wonderful holy site the next day, but Susan woke up with altitude sickness, which is often worse after sleeping. Forgoing the holy site, she rode a horse down about two thousand feet and then continued to ride along their planned route for the rest of that day. In another day, she felt better and began walking again.

A few days later, Susan and Linda spent some time in another small town. They visited a four-hundred-year-old Buddhist monastery, chatting with the lama and drinking tea with water buffalo milk. Later that evening they had dinner with some other western trekkers in a local teahouse. The trekkers carried on a lively and enthusiastic discussion of miles covered, athletic feats accomplished, the strife of crossing a high pass, and altitude sickness. Linda and Susan mentioned their time at the monastery earlier, and the whole table—seven people—said, "What monastery?" Not one of them had even noticed the temples in every town they had traveled through; they only stopped long enough to eat and sleep!

Halfway through the trip, Susan became very sick. One afternoon, she developed a ferocious headache, fever, and chills, all symptoms of a serious, possibly dangerous illness. Linda woke her off and on all night, making sure Susan was still conscious, and hoping she wasn't getting worse. Early the next morning, seeing no visible improvement, Linda went to locate their guide, Bhola, and find a way to get Susan to help. Frustrated that they had not let him know sooner, Bhola began a difficult search for a means to get Susan down the mountain. Although it was only 8:30 a.m., all of the men and horses had left the village hours before to work in the fields high in the mountains. After much searching, Bhola found a large basket, which he hitched to the back of Chotte Muktan, their porter, so that Susan could be carried down the mountain. A relay of three men managed over eight hours to get Susan through the mountains to the nearest doctor in the small village of Tato Pani. After another night of sleep and some antibiotics, Susan was weak but fine.

As Susan describes it, "I felt a bit humbled and amazed by the work of these men; a bit embarrassed at the effort they were making on my behalf; and very grateful that Linda was there. I knew that I was completely and utterly being taken care of and would be safe. The hardest part was that I felt sorry that the group had worked so hard to get me to safety, and then I seemed to be quite okay. I didn't doubt that I had needed help, but I felt scared and disappointed and grateful and a bit humble and embarrassed about it."

They rested in the paradise of Tato Pani for another two to three days, enjoying the hot springs at the base of the hill below their room and eating ripe oranges that just fell off the trees into their laps. The rest was wonderful, but they grew concerned about their impending departure. Because of the break that allowed Susan to recover from her illness, they no longer had any time to spare to get Linda to a road so she could catch her flight back to the States. The only way out with even a possibility of making it in time was to travel over the mountains—straight up, more than six thousand feet, for two days and then straight down for two more days. The doctor was still worried that at least some of Susan's illness had been related to the altitude, so she insisted that Susan descend immediately if she got any sort of headache at all. The group worked out a complicated contingency plan in case Susan's symptoms reappeared: Bhola and Susan would loop back and take a lower, slower route, and Linda and Chotte Muktan would continue on. All the plans were unnecessary as it turned out; Susan traveled well and Linda made her connections easily.

Susan's Reflections

"I traveled on the help of others—which was available to me because I had planned on the possibility of needing it, and because I am aware and accepting of my frailties. I traveled knowing that I had less than the requisite fortitude for the journey I wanted to take, and so I planned in compensations. Because of that, I had the wondrous sensation of really pushing my body, feeling my limits, and then having to go beyond them and then beyond them just a little more. I realized that I could get almost anywhere if I allowed myself to rest fully as I went along!

I went to Nepal hoping to walk in the tallest mountains on Earth in any way I could, for as long or as short a time as I could. It was almost beyond my dreams, given my limitations. I kept going by having the willingness to take care of myself at all times, and because I had a clear vision

that the purpose of this journey was joy. All I wanted to
accomplish was spiritual fulfillment, the rest didn't matter;
not passes, not peaks—just opening."

———

Susan's story radiates a quiet power illumined by her astonishing clarity about the real purpose of her journey: "the purpose of this journey was joy." Susan's clarity was so profound that being carried down the mountain in a basket on the back of a porter was incredibly *not* the defining moment of her journey! When we look back on significant moments in our lives, how many times have we been able to stay focused on our deepest goals? Or have we measured our success and happiness by external or irrelevant standards? Most of us have judged ourselves insufficient or incompetent far too often. We may have decided that our grandest moments were flawed because they did not live up to a Hollywood movie's idea of success. But imagine if we stopped measuring ourselves that way and instead decided to go on the adventure, fulfill a life dream, and stay focused on the joy. The truth is, once we make that decision, we have already succeeded.

Continuing to climb mountains with physical challenges and/or the limitations of an aging body is a complex process. Often, other qualities keep us going when life's trail suddenly gets rough, and we do not have the strength we thought we had. Determined to live our lives with passion and vitality, we can look to Susan's story, rich with ideas for how to accomplish a dream despite anticipated challenges.

First, we have to be prepared for the journey but also for setbacks, emotional and physical. More than prepare for setbacks, we have to plan on them. We are not oblivious to the things that can happen, but neither do we want to be paralyzed by fear of potential disasters. Instead we can accept our frailties and "plan in compensations."

Second, when we do hit a setback, we have to ask for help, and then we have to accept it. It sounds so simple, yet how do we deal with our pride? Susan's graceful acceptance of help and her ability to shift from humiliation and embarrassment to gratitude guide us. By planning on the need for help and accepting it when necessary, Susan was able to achieve an extraordinary goal, one that she would not have been able to accomplish by herself.

When we were younger, we might have held a strangely misguided belief that we had to do things all by ourselves for them to count as success. We may have felt that if we had help achieving our dreams and accomplishments, they would not feel like *ours*. They would belong to someone else as well; we would have to share. Here is the question: how many things have we *ever* done all by ourselves? Very few, actually. For nearly every accomplishment and achievement throughout our lives, we have been assisted by the power and strength of our families and communities. Sometimes that assistance was as easy as a foot rub or as strenuous as actually carrying us when we could not carry ourselves. As we look back on those times in our lives, it may inspire us to help someone else or to be part of someone else's climbing team. Here in Middlehood, perhaps we can start to put down our unrelenting pride and isolation, and instead be grateful for the power of community.

Third, we must take care of ourselves—every step of the way. No longer can we ignore our body or emotional needs. We may have done that as young women, but it is a recipe for disaster here in Middlehood. Being optimistic in Middlehood does not mean forgetting about the resources and supplies we are likely going to need somewhere along the way. If we are prone to sprained ankles, we will need to wear sturdy boots and pack a couple of elastic bandages. If we struggle with balance, a stout walking stick is a must. Maybe we did not need such tools in the past, but we might now. We could fail to accomplish a life goal if we do not have what we need. We have to keep our eye on the real prize and not get sidetracked by unimportant details.

Maybe the hardest part of climbing the mountain in Middlehood and beyond is deciding that we still *can* do it, can still choose a life full of opportunities for adventure and accomplishment. We may not be able to do things the way we used to, but that does not mean that we cannot do them at all. We cannot let our pride or fear get in the way. Instead we can realistically and honestly plan for our challenges by building in the support and resources we know we will need.

Regardless of whether we are strong or stumbling at any given moment, we have been climbing our mountain for a long time, and we know for sure that this journey cannot be accomplished in a mad dash or full-out sprint. Learning to pace ourselves has been incredibly important, and we can joyfully admit that some of the most precious parts of the journey are the moments when we took a break so that we could really appreciate the view.

Reflection Questions

- What is on my list of things I still want to do? What are my strengths? In what ways should I plan to compensate?
- How can other people—family and community—help me fulfill my dreams? How can I help others fulfill theirs?
- What things have I already done that I did not think I could do? What inspired me to do them?

CHAPTER 13

Life as a Mountain: Take a Step and Breathe

Be Bold. Envision yourself living a life that you love. Believe, even if you can only muster your faith for just this moment, believe that the sort of life you wish to live is, at this very moment, just waiting for you to summon it up. And when you wish for it, you begin moving toward it, and it, in turn, begins moving toward you.

~ Suzan-Lori Parks, *Mount Holyoke College, 2001 commencement address*

BY THE TIME WE HAVE LIVED forty or fifty or sixty years, we get it: life is the mountain. We are not beginners anymore, and we know that climbing this mountain is long and complex, with many different phases. It is a journey full of breathtaking views, arduous climbs, and profound accomplishments. Our stamina has been tested many times, and we have learned that sometimes we need to reach for a companion's hand to haul us up through a difficult patch. Other times, we have been delighted to stroll along by ourselves, with only our thoughts for company. We have cried in frustration as we unsuccessfully attempted to scramble through a section that seemed to have few obvious hand and footholds. We are no longer surprised that climbing up a mountain often requires us to descend into deep valleys. We may seem to be going in the wrong direction, but time and experience tell us that it is often the easiest and most direct path to reach a higher plateau.

We know how to assemble our gear with an eye for surprise weather changes, always bringing more than enough food and water, and not forgetting a map or GPS. All the while we remember that we have to carry our choices, so we give even more thought to what is necessary and what is luxury. After all of the thinking and choosing are done, we give a shrug and a laugh, because we are quite certain that no matter how much planning we do, there is no possible way to prepare for all that the mountain will bring to us. We must trust that we have prepared as well as we can and then go on the adventure.

The one thing we can count on is that life will demand everything we have, so we have learned to be strong in a variety of ways. We used to define being strong as having physical strength and determination, but here in Middlehood, we find that other kinds of strength—of character, of spirit—have become increasingly important. Here too, self-awareness, confidence, support, and faith make a huge difference in the success of our journey. But perhaps the most important survival tools we willingly carry in our backpacks are humor, love, and hope.

———

New York Hope by Nancy Geha

Several years ago, three devastating events happened to me almost simultaneously: I lost my job; a nine-year relationship ended; and I was facing the possible loss of my home. Right in the middle of all that, I was scheduled to go to New York for a conference. I was very depressed and hoped the trip would help me feel better, so I went. I attended the conference for only a short period of time, as being around so many people was hard while my life was falling apart.

It was winter in Manhattan, and the buildings blocked the sun, so I decided to take a walk in Central Park. I needed light and grass and trees. As I was walking toward the park, I noticed vendors on the sidewalk and was especially interested in a short, round man who was doing portraits in charcoal, chalk, and pencil. I decided that on my way back, I would ask him to do my portrait.

As I walked down the long, wide sidewalks in Central Park, I noticed what appeared to be a statue with wings at the end of the sidewalk. As I got closer, I saw that the statue was an angel on top of a fountain. Later, I found out that it was the Bethesda Fountain, and the statue was known as the Angel of the Waters. The angel held a lily that represents purity and was pointing downward toward the waters, blessing them. At her feet were four cherubs representing temperance, purity, health, and peace. Because it was winter, the fountain was off, and no one was around. I stood at her base and, with tears in my eyes, prayed for help, guidance, and healing. My prayer to the angel was, "I just want to know that everything will be okay." I said my prayer over and over. On my way back to the hotel, I looked for the artist I had seen earlier, but he was gone. Another disappointment.

The next day, I looked for the artist but could not find him and felt disappointed once again. I walked back to the fountain and repeated my prayer that everything would be okay. As I was returning to the hotel, I saw a sidewalk off to the left that led down a path to a place I couldn't see. On a whim, I decided to take the path and surprisingly came out at the Central Park Zoo. Lo and behold, sitting right outside the entrance to the Central Park Zoo was my artist, canvas poised, waiting for his next customer! My heart leaped with excitement at the thrill of having my portrait done.

As I talked to the artist about doing my portrait, I noticed that his bright blue eyes had a hazy covering, like cataracts. He spoke with an accent, and had marks on his neck indicating that he may have had treatment for cancer. For an hour, he drew my portrait and never spoke a word.

When he finished the portrait, he laid down his charcoal and said, "I want to tell you a story . . .

"There once was a man who committed a crime against his friend. He went to his friend and said, 'I need your forgiveness. I'll do anything for your forgiveness.'

"The friend responded, 'There is only one thing you can do to get my forgiveness. Hold out your hand; I will put this coin in the fire, get it red hot, take it out of the fire, and put it in the palm of your hand, and you will close your hand—a branding of sorts.'

"The man thought for a second and then said, 'I will do it. I need your forgiveness.'

"The friend then said, 'Close your eyes and hold out your hand.'

"Then he took the coin and laid it next to the fire but not in it, and used a stick to poke the fire. The friend then took the cold coin and put it in the man's hand and closed it. When the man opened his hand, what do you think he saw? A burn mark in the shape of a coin."

The artist asked me what I thought the moral of the story was. I was in no shape to guess. He then said, "If you truly believe that something will occur, if you truly believe that something will occur, the energy within you will make it so." He said it again: "If you truly believe that something will occur, the energy within you will make it so."

He said that he had signed the portrait and that it would be worth something someday. Then he showed it to me. When I was finished admiring it, he wrapped it up.

Just as I was about to leave, he took my hand and put his other hand on my shoulder. He looked in my eyes, his eyes now very clear, and said, "Everything will be okay, everything will be okay." The very words I had prayed less than an hour before, this man now said to me. I began to cry as I hugged him and then slowly walked away carrying my portrait.

When I returned to the hotel, I realized I had not even asked him his name nor seen his signature on the portrait. I opened it, and on the lapel of my coat he had signed a big white A.

Angels come in all shapes and sizes, and I wholeheartedly believe I was blessed with one.

Life did not get better immediately upon my return; that's not the way life is. But I went home with the one thing I needed desperately: hope. *A month later, my friend Ann called out of nowhere and offered me a job, the bank agreed to give me a loan for my home, and I began the healing process from the lost relationship. Along with my angel, I found faith, hope, and forgiveness, and the will to move on.*

———

Miracles don't always happen in a minute; sometimes they happen gently over time. But "if you truly believe that something will occur, the energy within you will make it so." Spiritual and wisdom traditions have always taught us this: what we believe, we will become, and what we value, we will collect and draw to ourselves.

There are many things in our lives that we cannot control, but we can control where we focus our attention. We can replay and repeat all of the sad, infuriating, unfair, traumatic things we have experienced, or we can remember and acknowledge them, and take action where we need to. We can choose to keep finding and focusing on moments of love and peace. We can do this only when we stay very present in our hours and days, really seeing the people, experiences, and possibilities around us.

This is the ultimate power we all have: to open our hearts and minds to an unknown path or an answer to a prayer that we never imagined. Again and again, life has asked us to close our eyes, hold out our hands, and be surprised. We have done that, sometimes in excitement, sometimes in fear, but if our lives have been rich with experiences, we have risked it and made our plans out of what landed.

With hindsight, we see that life has been a persistent teacher in the constant dance of evolution and revolution. We may love the part where our lives flowed along in easy and predictable ways, yet they likely were not the richest times of growth and change. Instead, we may look with quiet reflection on the times we were turned upside down by circumstances or events and realize that those moments changed our lives forever. We may have been pulled along kicking and screaming, but we met the challenges and learned what we needed to know.

Again and again we must renew our commitment to the way of the puma. If we deny our aging and fear the future, we will stop climbing and miss the power of what is yet to come. Instead, let us meet the challenges of Middlehood with courage, a growing sense of peace with our conflicts and limits, and a core of authenticity and commitment to our lives. These are the qualities that will carry us through Middlehood and into our elderhood, and none of them are dependent on our physical abilities, strength, or good looks!

Sometimes we need encouragement, and luckily, there are women all around us who generously share their insights born of life experiences. From the scree-covered trail of Mount Kilimanjaro, Reneé demonstrates the way to keep moving no matter how difficult the circumstances, while her mother, Sandra, assists us with her wise ability to gracefully make peace with her limits. In the mountain night, Cindy faces her wolves with a depth of courage that roars with inspiration, and Susan teaches us from the mountains of Nepal as she stands firm in her commitment to her life and dreams. We can draw strength and inspiration from these women, of course, but we can also look around and find hope and encouragement from our family and friends: a friend who knows sorrow and still lives with an open heart; a sister who pursues her art with passion and creativity; a mother determined to carry her family through financial hard times with laughter and love.

We all have stories, momentous and inconsequential, poignant and silly, that fill the book each of us has been writing throughout our life. Perhaps we used to think of our life as a collection of short stories, written in chronological order with permanent ink, each chapter a discrete, unconnected event or adventure. Nowadays, we know for sure that there is only one story in this book, and the chapters and tales are definitely not chronological. Instead, they constantly arrange and rearrange themselves in order of importance, the details changing from one reading to the next. Now we can understand that this is how the stories from our past have created our present story and how all of them, always changing and growing, will shape our lives in the future. Maybe only the stories that still fill us with guilt or shame do not change and have hardened into stone. Here in Middlehood, we understand that we must find a way to release even those stories.

When we are able to release them, we will see that the book we are writing is one of profound wisdom, full of love and guidance for ourselves and others. Each book is a love story, an adventure, and an exploration of philosophy and faith. Every story is the story of a woman who struggled, loved, laughed, dreamed, failed, and rose from the ashes; each tells the larger story of a life lived with meaning, courage, and love. Our stories contain the wisdom we seek, and we have only to look inside to find that we are becoming the wise women we have sought for so long.

We are experienced climbers and guides now, and we know how important it is to pace ourselves. We know to savor the precious moments when we can take a break and enjoy the view, because there will surely be challenges and surprises on the mountain trail ahead. So when the footing is uncertain, the air is thin, and the trail seems blocked by endless boulders, we take a step, then we stop and breathe for a bit, and then we take another step and breathe again . . .

ADDENDUM

The stories and life experiences included in this book have been amazing to read, but we know there are many more. We are planning additional books that will include stories on a variety of topics of interest to Middlehood women. If you are interested in submitting a story for a future book, please visit our website to find out about topics and guidelines. Remember that what you have learned through your experiences may help someone else in her journey.

For more information, to order books or schedule workshops and presentations, please visit our website: www.middlehood.com. We'd love to hear from you.

Blessings,
Nancy and Jane

INDEX

health ix–x, 7, 41–42, 48–49, 52, 55–59, 61–66, 88, 100, 136, 148, 156–157, 172, 178, 186, 193–194, 196, 205, 237, 242–243, 251

healthcare 56–65, 179, 193, 227

healthcare provider 57–65, 179

heart attack 38, 63–64

heart attacks 64

heart disease 59–60

heartwood 50

Henry, Cynthia xvii, 215

hepatitis B 185

hike 12, 100, 166, 208, 220, 241, 243

Himalayas 241

Hogan, Linda xvii, 212

hope xi, xv, xxii, 6, 9, 22–23, 25, 29, 31–32, 34, 37, 65, 68, 81, 104, 108, 112, 117, 123–124, 129, 137, 153, 155, 164, 170–171, 181–182, 194–195, 201, 204, 208, 221, 230, 234, 238, 250, 253, 255

hopeful 98, 104

hormone replacement therapy 61

hormones 36–37, 42–45, 57, 65, 120

"hormones talking" 42, 43, 65

Horombo Hut 12

hot flash xx, 39, 44, 46–47, 61, 100, 106, 121

hot flashes xx, 39, 44, 46–47, 61, 100, 121

husband 33, 45, 47, 52, 54, 56, 64, 68–69, 79, 97, 99–103, 111–113, 117–118, 121, 127–128, 139, 145–146, 150, 152, 179, 182, 184, 193, 206

hysterectomy 28

I

"I am who I always wanted to be" 87

in-between place 30, 110, 217

inspiration xxi, 226, 229, 255

inspirational xvi, 131

inspire xi, xv, 31, 99, 191, 229, 237, 247

inspires 191, 229

inspiring xx, 11, 231, 237

integrity 51, 201, 219

intimacy 54–55, 66, 102, 104, 106, 135

intimate 54–55, 99, 108, 110, 117, 127, 130, 156, 179

intimate relationships 55, 99, 108, 110, 117, 130

invisibility 25, 74, 79

invisible 2, 7, 76–78, 113, 131, 205

J

jaguar 166, 167

Japanese art 116

Jemison, Mae C. xvii, 1

jewel 214–215

jobs ix, 20, 30, 50, 60, 76, 85, 191, 193, 197, 202, 204,

Muktan, Chotte 244–245
mu'umu'u 71
"My Sister, Linda Sue" 185
Myss, Caroline xvi, 240

N

Nepal 241–242, 245, 255
"New York Hope" 250
New Zealand 19
Nigerian *gele* 71
Nogales, Ana xvi, 97
Northrup, Dr. Christiane ix, 44
Nye, Naomi Shihab xvii, 163

O

Obama, Michelle 74
obstacles xxi, 11, 16–17, 141, 196
O'Connor, Reneé xiii, xviii, 11,
    123–124, 255
O'Keeffe, Georgia xvi, 91
old-aged 2
oldful 3
"one step, one breath" 13, 114
Opalanga 178
orphan 133
osteoporosis 61

P

papa 81, 137, 140, 177, 185, 229
parent ix, xiii–xiv, xx, 7, 17, 22,
    51, 58–59, 64, 82, 98, 106,
    120–121, 124–125, 126,
    131, 131–149, 151, 153–154,
    158, 160–161, 163–164,
    169, 171–173, 176, 176–177,
    180, 183–184, 186–188,
        191–192, 195, 209–210,
        213, 233
Parkinson's 135
Parks, Suzan-Lori xviii, 249
partner xiii, xiv, 20, 22, 30, 33,
    51, 55–56, 58, 60, 64, 87,
    97, 99–103, 107–110, 112,
    116–118, 121, 126, 129,
    154, 172, 180, 184, 188,
    191, 225–226, 235
partners 22, 51, 55, 58, 64, 97,
    99, 101, 102, 103, 112, 172,
    188, 191, 235
passage ix, 4, 16, 21, 32, 50, 61,
    128, 164, 182, 208
passing 50, 71, 163, 175, 180,
    183, 186, 189, 194, 217
passing on 189
"pass through to a new
    beginning" 21, 32
path x, xxi, 10, 13, 19, 91, 97,
    110, 112–114, 117, 124, 168,
    171, 216, 219–224, 226,
    230, 233, 250–251, 254
Paulich, Dee v
peace xix, xxi, 28–29, 66, 122,
    129, 169, 178–179, 180, 181,
    195, 217, 219–220, 228,
    251, 254–255
peaceful xxi, 56
peak 11, 13–16, 87, 200, 246
peaks 11, 16, 246
perimenopausal 61
perimenopause ix, 39, 44–47, 62,
    63, 69, 79, 100, 121–122

CPSIA information can be obtained at www.ICGtesting.com
Printed in the USA
LVOW06s1824100813

347221LV00002B/3/P